Building a Foundation for Preschool Literacy

Effective Instruction for Children's Reading and Writing Development

2ND EDITION

CAROL VUKELICH
JAMES CHRISTIE

Part of the Preschool Literacy Collection edited by
Lesley Mandel Morrow

INTERNATIONAL
Reading Association
800 BARKSDALE ROAD, PO BOX 8139
NEWARK, DE 19714-8139, USA
www.reading.org

The International Reading Association attempts, through its publications, to provide a forum for a wide spectrum of opinions on reading. This policy permits divergent viewpoints without implying the endorsement of the Association.

Executive Editor, Books   Corinne M. Mooney
Developmental Editor   Charlene M. Nichols
Developmental Editor   Tori Mello Bachman
Developmental Editor   Stacey L. Reid
Editorial Production Manager   Shannon T. Fortner
Design and Composition Manager   Anette Schuetz
Project Editor   Stacey L. Reid

Cover   Design, Monotype; Photograph, ©2008 JUPITERIMAGES

Library of Congress Cataloging-in-Publication Data
Vukelich, Carol.
   Building a foundation for preschool literacy : effective instruction for children's reading and writing development / Carol Vukelich and James Christie. — 2nd ed.
       p. cm. — (Preschool literacy collection)
   Includes bibliographical references and index.
   ISBN 978-0-87207-700-3
   1. Language arts (Preschool)   I. Christie, James F.   II. Title.
   LB1140.5.L3V848 2009
   372.6--dc22   2008043189

We dedicate this book to the children, teachers, and project staff in our four Early Reading First projects who have taught us much:

- Delaware Early Reading First–New Castle County Head Start, Inc.—the Lambson, Rose Hill, and Manor Park centers
- Arizona Centers of Excellence in Early Education—Gadsden and Somerton school districts, Western Arizona Council of Governments Head Start, and Cocopah Head Start
- Opening Doors to Literacy–New Castle County Head Start, Inc.—the Absalom Jones, Marshallton, and Newark centers
- Mohave Desert Early Literacy Coalition—Bullhead City and Mohave Valley school districts and Western Arizona Council of Governments Head Start

CONTENTS

 Carol Vukelich is the Hammonds Professor in Teacher Education at the University of Delaware in Newark, Delaware, USA, where she teaches courses in literacy and directs the Delaware Center for Teacher Education. Her research interests include early literacy development, creating literacy strategies for young diverse learners, and coaching as professional development in early childhood settings. She is a coauthor of *Teaching Language and Literacy* (3rd ed.) and *Helping Young Children Learn Language and Literacy* (2nd ed.). She is also the coeditor of *Achieving Excellence in Preschool Literacy Instruction*.

Originally from northern Minnesota, Vukelich began her teaching career as a Head Start teacher in St. Cloud, Minnesota, USA. There she first recognized the importance of providing high-quality language and literacy instruction for all children, but particularly for children who have not received the rich literacy experiences needed to ensure their success in school and in life.

Vukelich has codirected two large Early Reading First projects: the Delaware Early Reading First project in New Castle, Delaware, and the Opening Doors to Literacy project in Wilmington, Delaware. Head Start teachers in both projects used the strategies described in this book; as a result, their students' language and early reading skills grew dramatically, and a majority of those children met the established spring benchmarks in language, print knowledge, and alphabet knowledge.

Vukelich has been a member of the International Reading Association (IRA) since the 1970s and has been president of Literacy Development in Young Children, an IRA special interest group. She also is a past president of the Association for Childhood Education International.

 James Christie is a Professor of Curriculum and Instruction at Arizona State University in Tempe, Arizona, USA, where he teaches courses in early childhood education and literacy. His research interests include early literacy development and children's play. He is a coauthor of *Teaching Language and Literacy* (3rd ed.), *Helping Young Children Learn Language and Literacy* (2nd ed.), *Play and Literacy in Early Education* (2nd ed.), and *Play, Development, and Early Education.*

Originally from central California, Christie began his teaching career as a kindergarten teacher in the Bakersfield City School District. That is where he initially became interested in the educational value of children's play. After receiving his doctorate at Claremont Graduate School, he has held faculty positions at the University of Kansas and Arizona State University.

Christie has codirected two large Early Reading First projects: the Arizona Centers of Excellence in Early Education in San Luis, Arizona, and the Mohave Desert Early Literacy Coalition project in Bullhead City, Arizona. Both projects place heavy emphasis on literacy-enriched play settings.

Christie has been a member of IRA since the late 1970s, and he currently is a member of the Association's Early Literacy Development Committee. He is also a member of the Board of Directors of Playing for Keeps and of the Scientific Advisory Board of the International Council for Children's Play. In addition, he is past president of The Association for the Study of Play and an editorial advisor for *Sesame Street* magazine.

GLOSSARY

This glossary provides definitions for many of the specialized literacy terms in this book. These terms are highlighted in boldface type on first occurrence.

assessment: Gathering relevant information to document a child's learning and growth.

concepts of print: Children's understandings about the functions (e.g., practical uses), structure (e.g., printed words are separated by spaces), and conventions (e.g., left-to-right, top-to-bottom sequence) of written language.

dialogic reading: An interactive form of storybook reading in which an adult helps a child become the storyteller.

dramatic play: An advanced form of play in which children take on roles and act out make-believe stories and situations.

emergent literacy: A perspective on early literacy development that contends that children construct their own knowledge about reading and writing as a result of social interaction and meaningful engagements with print.

environmental print: The print children see at home or in the community, including print on food containers and other kinds of product boxes, store signs, road signs, and advertisements.

formal assessment: Gathering information about learning during a special time set aside for testing using standardized tests.

informal assessment: Gathering information about learning while children engage in typical classroom activities.

literacy-enriched play settings: Play centers that are enhanced with appropriate theme-related literacy materials such as recipe cards, cookbooks, and food containers for the kitchen center.

phonemic awareness: The awareness of the individual sounds (phonemes) that make up spoken words.

phonological awareness: Awareness of the sounds of oral language.

print knowledge: Children's knowledge about printed letters, words, and book conventions (such as title, author, illustrator, reading from left to right and from top to bottom).

scientifically based reading research (SBRR): An approach to early literacy instruction that is based on rigorous experimental research and focuses on explicit instruction on the skills and concepts that are the best predictors of later reading achievement.

shared reading: A classroom strategy in which a teacher reads a Big Book with enlarged print and encourages the children to read along on parts that they can remember or predict. Shared reading models the reading process and draws children's attention to print concepts and letter knowledge.

shared writing: A strategy in which the teacher writes down children's own stories about their everyday experiences. These highly contextualized stories are easy for children to read and can be used to teach concepts of print.

specific indicators: Specific statements of what preschool children should know and be able to do.

standards: Statements that define what children should know and be able to do in a particular area such as literacy or mathematics.

writing center: A classroom area stocked with materials that invite children to engage in writing.

CHAPTER 1

How Children Learn to Read and Write

Currently, there are two main theoretical perspectives on early reading and writing: **emergent literacy** and **scientifically based reading research** (SBRR). In the sections that follow, we briefly review the key beliefs and the research base of each of these diverging views of early literacy development and teaching. Next, we present our position that these two views should be blended together so that children can benefit from the best strategies in each perspective. We then highlight eight basic principles of effective early literacy instruction.

Emergent Literacy

During the 1980s and 1990s, emergent literacy (a term coined by Marie Clay in 1966) became the dominant theoretical perspective in the field of early reading and writing. According to this social constructivist view, literacy acquisition has much in common with oral language development. Children begin learning about reading and writing at a very early age by observing and interacting with adults and other children as they use literacy in everyday activities, such as writing shopping lists, and in special literacy-focused routines, such as storybook reading. On the basis of these observations and activities, children construct their own concepts about the functions and structure of print and then try these in play (e.g., pretending to read a favorite book to a doll) and in everyday situations (e.g., recognizing a favorite brand of cereal at the supermarket). Young children test their beliefs about how written language works and, based on how others respond and the results they get, modify these beliefs and construct more sophisticated systems of reading and writing. For example, their attempts at writing often evolve from scribbles, to letter-like forms, to random streams of letters, and finally to increasingly elaborate systems of invented spelling (Sulzby, 1990). Eventually, with lots of opportunities to engage in meaningful literacy activities, large amounts of interaction with adults and peers, and some incidental instruction, children become conventional readers and writers.

The emergent literacy perspective is based on several strands of research. We will briefly review some key findings from these studies. For more specific information and research citations, we recommend that readers consult the integrative reviews published in Volumes II and III of the *Handbook of Reading Research* (Sulzby & Teale, 1991; Yaden, Rowe, & MacGillivray, 2000) or a comprehensive early childhood language arts textbook (Morrow, 2009; Vukelich, Christie, & Enz, 2008).

Several pioneering emergent literacy studies focused on early readers, children who came to kindergarten already able to read some words (Clark, 1976; Durkin, 1966). Results showed that many early readers were of average intelligence, contradicting the commonly assumed link between early reading and intellectual giftedness. Parental interviews revealed that these children shared several characteristics, including an early interest in print and writing. The parents also reported that they frequently read stories to their children and took the time to answer their children's questions about written language. These findings suggested that home experiences had an important role in promoting early reading.

Concepts of Print

Research on early readers stimulated interest in what typical preschool-age children were learning about literacy. Many of these early studies focused on children's **concepts of print**: children's understandings about the functions, structure, and rules of written language. For example, researchers discovered that many 3-year-olds come to expect print to be meaningful. This understanding becomes evident when children point to words on signs, cereal boxes, or menus and ask, "What does that say?" Or, after making marks on a piece of paper, they ask, "What did I write?"

Research also revealed that young children quickly discover that print is functional and can be used to get things done in everyday life. For example, many 3-year-olds are familiar with the purposes of different types of print, such as store signs, restaurant menus, and name labels on presents. Young children's knowledge of the functional uses of literacy also is demonstrated during **dramatic play**. Researchers have reported numerous incidents of preschoolers engaging in a variety of functional literacy activities while engaging in dramatic play, including jotting down phone messages, writing checks to pay for purchases, looking up recipes in cookbooks, and making shopping lists.

> Young children quickly discover that print is functional and can be used to get things done in everyday life.

Environmental Print

Other researchers studied young children's ability to recognize **environmental print**—print that occurs in real-life contexts. Results showed that many 3- and 4-year-olds can identify product labels (Colgate, Cheerios, Pepsi), restaurant signs (McDonald's, Pizza Hut), and street signs (STOP) (McGee, Lomax, & Head, 1988). Children often begin to recognize the letters of the alphabet at about the same time as they "read" environmental print. This ability varies considerably among children, with some children recognizing up to a third of the alphabet by age 3 and others not learning any letters until age 5. Children's own names and highly salient environmental print are often the source of initial letter learning. Baghban (1984), for example, describes how *K* (K-Mart), *M* (McDonald's), and *G* (Giti) were among the first letters recognized by her 2-year-old daughter, Giti.

Developmental Trends

Another strand of emergent literacy research focused on developmental trends in early forms of reading and writing. For example, Sulzby (1990) asked preschool children to write stories and then to read what they had written. Based on this research, Sulzby identified seven broad categories of early writing: (1) drawing as writing, (2) scribble writing, (3) letter-like units, (4) nonphonetic letter strings, (5) copying from environmental print, (6) invented spelling, and (7) conventional writing. Sulzby discovered that, while there is a general movement from less mature forms toward more conventional forms, children move back and forth across these types of writing when composing texts and often combine several different types in the same composition. Sulzby (1985) also found that children's storybook-reading behaviors appear to follow a developmental pattern, with their attention gradually shifting from the pictures to aspects of print. In addition, the intonation of children's voices when reading gradually shifts from sounding like they are telling an oral story to sounding like they are reading.

Home Environment

A fourth and final strand of emergent literacy research focused on young children's home environments in an attempt to discover factors that promote early literacy learning. These studies have revealed four groups of home factors that are particularly important in getting children off to a good start in learning to read and write.

Access to Print and Books. Literacy learning is facilitated when young children have easy access to books and opportunities to see lots of print. For example, plentiful home supplies of children's books have been found to be associated with early reading and interest in literature. It is also beneficial when parents and other caregivers take children to libraries and bookstores.

Adult Demonstrations of Literacy Behavior. When children see their family members use print for various purposes—writing shopping lists, paying bills, and writing notes to each other—they begin to learn about the practical uses of written language and to understand why reading and writing are activities worth doing. If their parents happen to model reading for pleasure, so much the better.

Supportive Adults. Early readers tend to have parents or other caregivers who are very supportive of their early attempts at literacy. While these adults rarely attempt to directly teach children how to read and write, they do support literacy growth through activities such as the following:

- Reading aloud storybooks frequently
- Answering children's questions about print
- Pointing out letters and words in the environment
- Providing easy access to print materials
- Providing children with a wide variety of experiences such as trips to stores, parks, and museums
- Initiating functional literacy activities such as suggesting that a child write a letter to Grandma or help make a shopping list

Storybook Reading. Research has consistently shown that parent–preschooler storybook reading is positively related to outcomes such as language growth, early literacy, and later reading achievement (Bus, van IJzendoorn, & Pellegrini, 1995). Other studies have identified ways in which storybook reading facilitates literacy growth (Barrentine, 1996; Durkin, 1966; Holdaway, 1979; Snow & Ninio, 1986). These ways include the following:

- Building positive attitudes about books and reading
- Providing children with a model of skilled reading

- Creating a context in which parents can informally teach vocabulary and concepts and provide support for children's early attempts at reading
- Encouraging independent engagements with literacy by familiarizing children with stories and encouraging them to attempt to read the stories on their own

Early childhood language arts programs based on the emergent literacy perspective feature experiences that are similar to those that children have in enriched home environments—print-rich classrooms, frequent storybook reading, demonstrations of various forms and functions of literacy, and many opportunities for children to engage in meaningful reading and writing activities. These types of emergent literacy experiences build on what children have already learned about written language, provide a smooth transition between home and school, and promote initial success with learning to read and write. Because reading aloud to children has been shown to be "the single most important activity" in building a foundation for learning to read (Adams, 1990, p. 46), we will return to this topic in Chapter 4 and explore **shared reading** in detail.

Shared Writing: An Emergent Literacy Strategy

Shared writing, also referred to as the Language Experience Approach, involves having children read texts composed of their own oral language. Children first dictate a story about a personal experience, and the teacher writes it down. The teacher reads the story back to the children and then gives them an opportunity to read it. This can be done with groups of children using the chalkboard or chart paper, or with individuals using regular writing paper.

Shared writing is an excellent way for teachers to demonstrate the relationship between oral and written language. It helps children to realize that what they say can be written down in print and that print can be read back as oral language.

Shared writing also presents opportunities for teachers to demonstrate the structure and conventions of written language. The children watch as the teacher spells words conventionally, leaves spaces between words, uses a left-to-right and top-to-bottom sequence, starts sentences and names with capital letters, and ends sentences with periods or other terminal punctuation marks. Through these demonstrations, children can observe how the mechanical aspects of writing work.

The shared writing strategy has the additional advantage of making conventional writing and reading easier for children. By acting as scribe, the teacher removes mechanical barriers to written composition. The children's compositions are limited only by their oral language and experiential backgrounds. Reading is also made much easier because shared writing stories are composed of the children's own oral language and based on their personal experiences. This close personal connection with the story makes it easy for children to predict the identity of unknown words in the text. The vignette that follows shows what shared writing may look like in the classroom. (In this example and many classroom examples in this book, all student and teacher names are pseudonyms or represent composite descriptions of exemplary teaching and learning we've seen in our classrooms.)

●　●　●　●　●　●　●　●　●　●　●　●　●　●

Strategies in Use: Shared Writing

Preschool teacher Linda Lopez links shared reading with storybook reading. She had just finished reading the Big Book *There Was an Old Lady Who Swallowed a Fly* by Simms Taback (2000). Her class loved listening to the story, and Linda decided to take advantage of the children's enthusiasm by following up with a shared writing activity in which the children write a letter to the "Old Lady." Linda starts the lesson by asking who wants to write such a letter. Almost all of the children raise their hand and shout out "Me! Me!" Linda has already written the beginning of the letter at the top of a large piece of chart paper. She reads this to the children: "Dear Old Lady…" Then she asks the children what they want to say next.

The children are very concerned about the Old Lady's eating habits, so they proceed to dictate sentences telling her what *not* to eat: lots of candy, spiders, cows, and so on. Linda writes down each child's comments, reading each word as she writes it. She also re-reads each sentence when it is finished.

During this dictation phase, several children make comments about the print. For example, one child exclaims that the word *eat* starts with the letter *t*. Linda takes advantage of this teachable moment and sounds out the word (/ē - t/) and points out that it does contain a /t/ sound, but that it comes at the end of the word rather than at the beginning. She also points out that *eat* starts with the /ē/

sound and asks which letter represents that sound. This teaches the children two key skills: **phonemic awareness** and letter–sound associations.

After the children have dictated all the things that the Old Lady should not eat, Linda asks if they want to put anything else in their letter. Several children mention that the Old Lady needs to eat healthy food. So Linda concludes the story with this positive recommendation. One of the children helps with the spelling, pointing out that *healthy* starts with an *h*. Linda then rereads the story:

> Dear Old Lady,
> Don't eat a fly and don't eat lots of candy.
> Don't eat all of the animals.
> Don't eat a cow.
> Don't eat a spider.
> You should eat healthy foods.

Then Linda writes, "From your friend," and reads it to the class. One of children suggests that they should all sign the letter so that the Old Lady knows who the letter is from. Linda responds this is a good idea. All of the children then take turns writing their names at the end of the letter. Finally, Linda reads the complete letter one more time, including the children's names. The children have figured out what the print says by this point and are able to read along fluently with Linda.

• • • • • • • • • • • • • •

Scientifically Based Reading Research

During the late 1980s and the 1990s, when the emergent literacy perspective was the prevailing view in early childhood education, another very different view of beginning literacy was gaining momentum, primarily in the fields of educational psychology and special education. This movement, commonly referred to as SBRR, asserts that rigorous experimental research can reveal (a) the skills and concepts that young children need to master to become proficient readers and writers and (b) the most effective strategies for teaching this content.

Whereas emergent literacy has relied primarily on qualitative forms for research, the SBRR perspective uses correlational studies and tightly controlled, quantitative experiments; hence the label *scientifically based*

(Christie, 2008). And while emergent literacy advocates place heavy value on the social and meaning-based aspects of literacy, SBRR has focused more on decoding print and on visual and auditory aspects of the reading process (Rayner, Foorman, Perfetti, Pesetsky, & Seidenberg, 2002). Reading for understanding is still the ultimate objective of instruction, but SBRR advocates believe that children must first master the skills that enable them to process print before comprehension becomes possible.

The SBRR perspective first was introduced in Adams's (1990) landmark book, *Beginning to Read: Thinking and Learning About Print*. Adams introduced the concept of basing instruction on research about what young children need to know to be successful readers and put considerable stress on understanding of the alphabetic principle that letters represent the sounds in words. The SBRR movement gained momentum with the publication of *Preventing Reading Difficulties in Young Children* (Snow, Burns, & Griffin, 1998). Snow and her colleagues emphasized using empirical evidence or "science" to discover (a) strong predictors of success and failure in reading and (b) effective strategies for preventing reading difficulties. More recently, the U.S. Department of Education has used the SBRR perspective as the foundation for many initiatives, including Good Start, Grow Smart and the Early Reading First grant program. Early Reading First projects are designed to increase the school readiness of low-income children by providing them with print-rich environments and scientifically based early reading instruction.

> The SBRR movement has identified the core knowledge and skills young children must develop to become successful readers.

Perhaps the most valuable contribution of the SBRR movement is that it has identified the core knowledge and skills young children must develop to become successful readers. Longitudinal studies have shown that preschool-age children's oral language (expressive and receptive language, including vocabulary development), **phonological awareness**, and alphabet knowledge are predictive of reading achievement in the elementary grades (Snow et al., 1998). Print awareness, which includes concepts of print (e.g., understanding how print can be used) and conventions of print (e.g, left-to-right, top-to-bottom sequence), has been found to be positively correlated with reading ability in the primary grades. As mentioned earlier, these concepts about print also received considerable attention from emergent literacy researchers.

SBRR investigators have also focused on identifying effective strategies for teaching this core literacy content to young children. One of the most consistent research findings is that young children's phonological awareness and alphabet knowledge can be increased via explicit instruction (National Institute of Child Health and Human Development [NICHD], 2000; Snow et al., 1998). This instruction often takes the form of games and other engaging activities, but it also contains teacher modeling and explicit teaching, guided practice, and independent practice.

Phonemic Awareness Instruction: An SBRR Strategy

SBRR has made several important contributions to the field of early literacy, including identifying key knowledge and skills that young children need to learn to be successful in learning to read. In addition, SBRR has identified developmental sequences for some of these skills and effective explicit-instruction teaching strategies.

Phonemic awareness—children's awareness of the individual sounds that make up spoken words—is a good example. Research has shown that phonemic awareness in kindergarten is a strong predictor of future reading achievement, and that direct instruction in phonemic awareness exerts strong, positive effects on reading and spelling development (Dickinson, McCabe, Anastasopoulos, Peisner-Feinberg, & Poe, 2003; NICHD, 2000). In addition, researchers have identified a developmental sequence that can help guide this instruction. Before young children can become aware of phonemes, they first must master phonological awareness and learn to recognize larger units of oral language, including words and syllables (Adams, 1990). Once they have mastered the understanding that speech comprises words and syllables, they can then begin to develop phonemic awareness, including the ability to analyze, synthesize, and manipulate the phonemes that make up words.

Research suggests a sequence of instructional activities that starts by building the broader concepts of phonological awareness and then moves toward awareness and manipulation of phonemes (Adams, Foorman, Lundberg, & Beeler, 1998).

Rhyming.   These activities focus children's attention on the ending sounds of words. For example, children recite or sing well-known nursery rhymes such as "Jack and Jill." Once children are familiar with a rhyme, the teacher repeats it, leaving out a rhyming word, and asks the children to guess the missing rhyming words, as in, "Jack and Jill went up a ___" (Ericson & Juliebö, 1998).

Segmenting Words.   These activities develop children's awareness that language is made up of strings of words. For example, the teacher can have children push a chip to represent each word in a sentence. For example, the teacher could say "Fuzzy Wuzzy was a bear" very slowly. The children would push out a chip as each of the five words is spoken.

Segmenting Syllables.   These activities develop children's ability to segment words into separate syllables. For example, the teacher can help children clap the syllables in each child's first name: *Ann* (clap), *Joe* (clap), *Su-zy* (clap, clap), *Jua-ni-ta* (clap, clap, clap). After each name has been clapped, the teacher can ask the children how many syllables they heard.

Sound Matching.   These activities ask children to decide which of several words begins with a specific sound. For example, the teacher shows children several pictures of familiar objects (dog, horse, elephant) and asks which begins with the /d/ sound.

Initial and Final Sounds.   In these activities, children are given words and asked to tell which sound occurs at the beginning or end. For example, the children are asked, "What's the sound that starts these words: *run, rabbit, roar?*"

Phonemic Blending.   In these activities, children are asked to combine individual sounds to form words. For example, the teacher can tell the class that she is thinking of a small animal. Then she says the name of the animal in separate phonemes (/k/, /a/, /t/) and asks the class to guess the identity of the animal. This requires children to blend individual phonemes to produce the name of the animal (Yopp, 1992).

Phonemic Segmentation.   This is the opposite of blending. Here, the teacher asks children to break up words into individual sounds (*cat* becomes /k/, /a/, /t/). Calkins (1994) calls the ability to segment words "rubber-banding"—stretching words to hear the individual phonemes.

Phonemic Manipulation.   This more difficult phonemic awareness task requires children to mentally add, delete, substitute, or reverse phonemes in words. For example, the teacher can ask children to say a word and then say it again without the initial sound (*pant-ant, fog-og*) or to substitute one sound with another (put /ă/ in the middle of *sud* and the word becomes *sad*).

An Alternative Developmental Sequence

More recent research has questioned Adams and colleagues' (1998) sequence. Lonigan (2008) describes a sequence based on his research that proceeds from word awareness, to syllable awareness, to onset-rime awareness, to phoneme awareness. From his research, Lonigan also provides a description of end-of-preschool expectations. For example, he reports that by the end of preschool years, 80% of children can blend two words to make a new word (e.g., *cow* and *boy* = *cowboy*); 80% of children can blend two syllables to make a word (e.g., *can* and *dee* = *candy*); and 20% of children can blend phonemes to produce a word (e.g., /k/, /a/, /t/ = *cat*). Lonigan's sequence, then, suggests that over the preschool years children proceed toward smaller and smaller units (e.g., from words in a sentence to syllables in words to sounds in words), from detection (e.g., picking two words that begin with the same sound) to production (e.g., saying two words that begin with the same sound), and from blending the phonemes into words (e.g., /k/, /a/, /t/ = *cat*) to eliding or separating the phonemes (e.g., *cat* = /k/, /a/, /t/). While Lonigan proposes a different developmental sequence, the activities described above nonetheless are appropriate.

An explicit instruction approach can be used with these activities: The teacher models how to do the activity, provides guided practice, and finally presents opportunities for independent practice. For example, during large-group time, the teacher can demonstrate how to clap the syllables in a name. Then the children take turns clapping the syllables in their names, with help from the teacher. Finally, children can pick a partner and practice clapping syllables in their names and their friends' names on their own.

SBRR researchers have also recommended a number of other research-based teaching ideas such as the ones set forth here:

- Engaging children in extended discussions and exposing them to words
- Print-rich classroom environments
- Interactive storybook-reading techniques such as **dialogic reading**
- **Literacy-enriched play centers**

Neuman (2002) provides a concise review of these teaching strategies. We describe several SBRR strategies below in the next section and in subsequent chapters.

Blended Early Literacy Instruction

Our position on these two perspectives on early reading and writing is quite simple. We believe that emergent literacy and SBRR need to be blended together to provide young children with balanced, effective early literacy instruction. Both views make significant contributions to a well-rounded early literacy program. Children need meaningful, social engagements with books, various forms of print, and writing. In addition, most children also need some explicit, developmentally appropriate instruction on vocabulary, phonological awareness, alphabet knowledge, and print awareness.

By combining the emergent literacy and SBRR perspectives, we have developed eight basic principles of effective early literacy instruction.

1. *Early language and literacy education should focus on core content— the knowledge, skills, and dispositions that are predictive of later success in learning to read and write.* This core content includes oral language, phonological awareness, alphabet knowledge, and print awareness. Focusing on this core content will ensure that instructional time is being used optimally to promote children's academic readiness.

2. *Oral language lays the foundation for early literacy development.* Unfortunately, which words to teach is not clearly defined in early literacy pedagogy (Roskos et al., 2008). Some say that teachers should engage children in rich conversations and expose them to rare words that are not encountered in everyday speech (Roskos, Tabors, & Lenhart, 2009). For instance, when studying transportation, children can be introduced to the names of different vehicles (e.g., pickup trucks, oil tankers, and airplanes), transportation occupations (e.g., taxi driver, truck driver, and mechanic), and transportation-related tools (e.g., tire pressure gauge, hydraulic lift). When such keywords are incorporated into daily activities, children come to know their meanings. Others say that teachers should teach words "of high frequency for mature language users and are found across a variety of domains" (Beck, McKeown, & Kucan, 2002, p. 8). Words like *curious* and *protect* are examples of these kinds of words, words Beck and colleagues call Tier 2 words. Still others (e.g., Biemiller, 2005) argue for the development of root words that are taken mainly from Dale and Chall's (1948) readability index. So teachers' first challenge is to select the words they will teach.

3. *Storybook reading is the cornerstone of early literacy instruction.* Children need to be read to frequently—in large groups and small groups, with little books and Big Books, and using a variety of texts, including

storybooks, informational books, and poetry. Children should actively engage in these reading sessions, making predictions, asking questions, offering their reactions and opinions, and having opportunities to participate in book-related activities.

4. *A carefully planned classroom environment enables literacy development to flourish.* Teachers should provide children with a print-rich classroom environment that will encourage children to engage in emergent forms of reading and writing. There should be a well-stocked library center, a **writing center**, many examples of functional print, and **literacy-enriched play settings**. In addition, the day should be scheduled with sensitivity to young children's learning and developmental needs, providing large blocks of time for individual and small-group activities and shorter amounts of time for whole-group, teacher-led activities.

5. *Children need opportunities to engage in emergent forms of reading and writing.* Children should have opportunities to explore the books that are read during storybook-reading sessions and to engage in functional reading (e.g., attendance lists, calendars, daily schedules) and writing activities (e.g., sign-up sheets for popular learning centers). There also should be opportunities for them to incorporate literacy into their play activities.

6. *Developmentally appropriate forms of explicit instruction should be used to teach core literacy concepts and skills.* Teachers can teach many concepts of print while engaging children in shared reading. For example, they can use a pointer to model the left-to-right and top-to-bottom sequence of written language and then invite children to use the pointer—first with some support, and later on their own with a partner. Rhymes, songs, and games can be used to teach important phonological awareness skills.

7. *Teachers need to help parents support their children's language, reading, and writing development.* Many parents and other primary caregivers underestimate the importance of their role in helping their children become competent language users and successful readers. Teachers must discover ways to work with their students' parents to ensure the development of confident readers and writers. Given the variety of family structures today, *parent* must be broadly defined. In some families, the "parent" may be an older sibling, or a grandparent, or foster parents, or two moms. The key is for the teacher to connect with the people who are significant in each child's life.

8. *Oral language and early literacy instruction and* **assessment** *should be guided by* **standards** *that define the knowledge and skills young children need to become successful readers and writers.* Most U.S. states have adopted

early learning standards for prekindergarten students. These research-based guidelines define what children in that state should know and be able to do before entering kindergarten. Teachers must be aware of their state's standards and must use them as guides in planning their daily instruction and in assessing their students' learning.

The Principles of Effective Early Literacy Instruction in Action

In the following chapters, we provide a rich description of these eight principles in action. Chapter 2 explains how classroom environments can be a powerful catalyst to literacy learning, and Chapter 3 describes how teachers can plan a daily schedule that meets children's needs and integrates language and literacy into all components of the curriculum. Chapter 4 focuses on effective strategies for reading books to young children, and Chapter 5 discusses ways in which teachers can partner with parents to promote early literacy learning. Finally, Chapter 6 explains how young learners can be provided with opportunities to study meaningful topics and learn key literacy skills at the same time. This chapter also discusses how early learning standards can be linked with assessment and instruction. In addition, there are two appendixes: Appendix A contains a list of props for use in literacy-enriched dramatic play centers, and Appendix B presents a compilation of state preschool standards for language and literacy.

PROFESSIONAL DEVELOPMENT FOR PRE- AND INSERVICE TEACHERS

This chapter discusses the two major views of early reading and writing—emergent literacy and SBRR—and makes the argument that the two approaches should be blended together.

1. Jot down a brief description of how you teach reading and writing to preschoolers, or if you are not yet teaching, visit a nearby preschool and make a list of how that teacher teaches literacy. Code each item on your list according to perspective: EL for emergent literacy and SBRR for scientifically based reading research. Which perspective do you (or the teacher that you visited) favor? Are you (or the other teacher) using a blended approach?

2. Access your state's Department of Education website and bookmark your state's early literacy standards. Compare what your state expects

preschool children to know with what a neighboring state expects pre-schoolers to know. How do both states' standards match up with your own expectations for preschoolers' literacy abilities?

3. Access the U.S. Department of Education website for Early Reading First (www.ed.gov/programs/earlyreading/index.html). List three things you learned about Early Reading First that surprised you. Are there any Early Reading First–funded programs in your area? Arrange to visit the nearest program.

CHAPTER 2

Creating a Literacy-Rich Environment for Young Children

Think about the preschool classroom that you know best. Does it look like the classroom in Figure 1 or Figure 2? What are the differences between these two classrooms? One of the two has the appearance of a classroom designed to support children's learning. Which one? Why?

If you selected Figure 2 as the better designed preschool classroom, congratulations! The teacher who created this classroom environment used the principles we will discuss in this chapter to create a quality place for young children to play and learn.

Designing the Classroom Environment: What the Research Says

Neuman and Roskos (2007) are known widely for their research on creating quality learning environments for young children. According to their research, teachers organize their classrooms and carve the classroom space into areas for work and play influences their young learners' behavior. They indicate that print-rich classroom environments (i.e., paper, writing tools, books, posters, signs embedded everywhere in the classroom) invite children to learn about print, and that when the library corner, writing center, and dramatic play center are well-equipped and well-organized, children's development and learning are supported. They also conclude that teachers play an important role in children's development, and that the classroom environment is more than physical space and materials. The amount and quality of adult–child talk are key components of the classroom environment.

Arranging the Classroom

In designing a learning environment for young children, bigger is not always better. We recommend that teachers divide the large, open classroom space into small centers. Small, well-defined spaces encourage children to

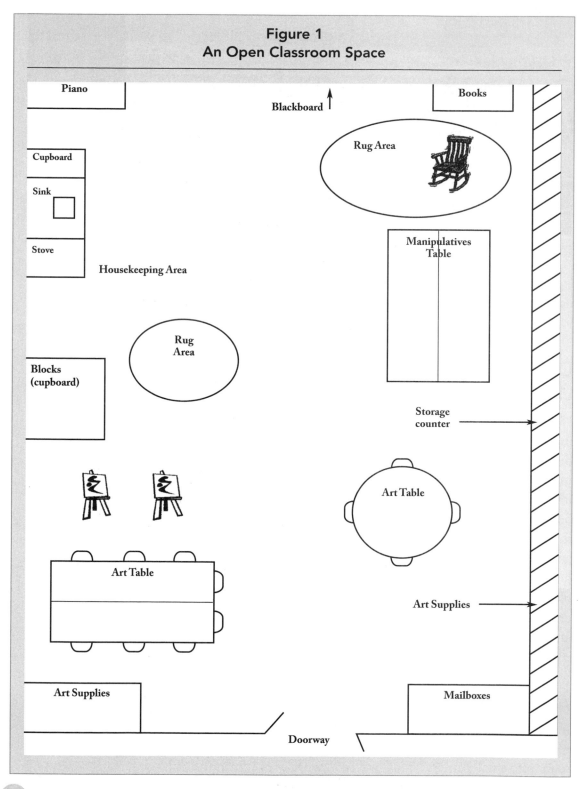

Figure 1
An Open Classroom Space

Figure 2
Classroom Space Divided Into Centers

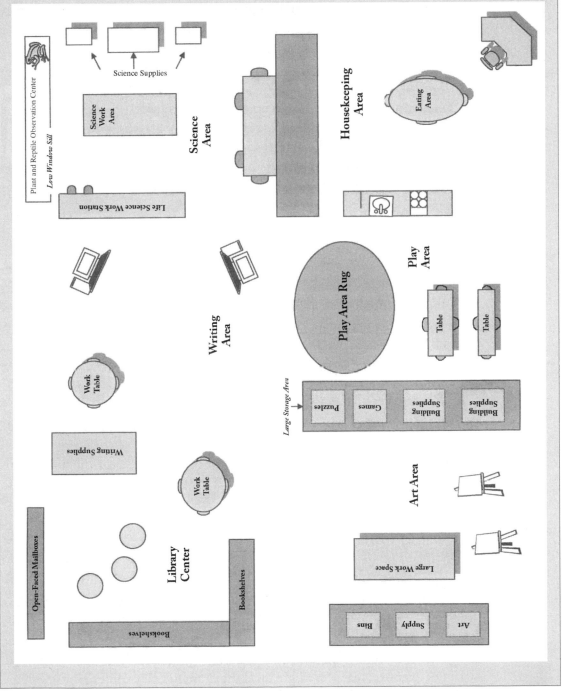

focus on the materials at hand, interact with other children, and persist in their play activities. When young children enter a learning center, they first explore and examine the materials. Exploration is followed by more complex, meaningful play. Research has shown that when the space is snug but not cramped, with room enough for five or six children, children's play becomes more complex and more meaningful, and their play lasts for a longer time (DeLong et al., 1994).

Creating Defined Play Spaces or Centers

Classroom furniture such as bookshelves and tables can serve as dividers to define the play centers. Chart stands, puppet stages, artificial trees, and housekeeping props, such as wooden ovens and refrigerators, can also serve this purpose. When the boundaries of each play area are marked clearly, children discover how to use the play space more effectively.

Arranging Furniture Within Each Center to Encourage Interaction

Children can learn from one another as they play in each center. To encourage children to play together, Han and Christie (2001) advise teachers to group the chairs to facilitate conversation and to provide multiple sets of props. Placing pairs of chairs in front of classroom computers encourages children to collaborate while using the computer to play games, get information, and write texts.

Placing Related Centers Near Each Other

If the writing center is next to the library center, children will be encouraged to write about the books they are reading. The science center should be near the mathematics center, and the block center near the housekeeping center. Placing similar centers near each other encourages children to use a variety of materials to support their explorations.

Using Print to Define Centers

Some features of the classroom in Figure 2 cannot be seen from an aerial perspective. Looking directly into a center makes other important features visible. Notice how, in Figure 3, the teacher has used print to define the types of activities that should occur in the area. First, the teacher used a sign to label the center. She thought a great deal about what to name the center because it is important to use labels that children will understand. For example, teachers might label the dramatic play center Housekeeping

**Figure 3
The Writing Center**

Center, Dress-Up Corner, or Home Corner. Such labels help define the purpose of the center for the children. The Housekeeping Area is a place for children to play what they see happening in their home. The Dress-Up Corner is a place to wear dress-up clothes. Similarly, teachers might label the library center Book Corner or Reading Corner. Prior to coming to pre-school, some young children will have little or no experience with libraries. Using a label like Book Corner makes it clear that this center is a place for reading books.

Next, the teacher hung the sign low, at the children's eye level, and put pictures next to the label. A picture helps the children "read" the print and gives purpose for their play in the area. Such strategies gently coax the children to engage in behaviors appropriate to the center's activity.

The teacher also added functional signs to the center. "Write Books Here" encourages the children to use the small blank books to write their stories, and "Open" indicates that the center is available for play today.

Finally, the teacher labeled the materials storage places and added a picture next to the print. These labels, with pictures, help the children to find the needed materials and to return the used materials to their appropriate places—making clean-up time much easier for the teacher and the children. Notice also how similar materials (paper, writing tools) are grouped together to help the children see categories of materials.

Including Environmental Print

Another way to enrich the classroom literacy environment is to bring in lots of environmental print that children see in their lives outside the classroom—print such as *STOP*, *McDonald's*, and *Cheerios*. Many young children learn to "read" this kind of print through their many experiences with it. The research on children's reading of environmental print suggests that children use context to help them read the word (Ehri & Roberts, 2006). That is, at the grocery store, they point and demand, "I want that one—Cheerios!" They seem able to read the word *Cheerios*. However, when *Cheerios* is cut off the box and the picture is removed, children no longer can read the word; they need the whole cereal box in full color with the picture to read *Cheerios*. By themselves, experiences with environmental print do not result in children learning to read. However, learning to read environmental print does help children learn to expect print to have meaning and to know that groups of letters make up something that can be read.

When teachers add labels to the classroom environment and point them out as part of the daily routine, children's knowledge of print grows. Classroom labels become as familiar and meaningful as the logos and street signs found throughout the community.

• • • • • • • • • • • • • • • •

Strategies in Use: Including Environmental Print in the Classroom

Andre waits by the classroom door for his friends to join him. He looks up at the "Exit" sign above the door. He turns to his teacher and says, "I know what that says: Go outside." (He makes *outside* two words, *out* and *side*.) As he says each word, he points to a letter. But one letter remains. He corrects himself. "Oh no, it says, Go out side here."

• • • • • • • • • • • • • • • •

Designing Learning Centers

Ecological psychologists have researched the importance of the environment on behavior and learning (Barker, 1978; Smith & Connolly, 1980). A conclusion from these researchers' work is that children's behavior is greatly influenced by the classroom environment. Teachers who want children to behave like readers and writers must create a classroom environment that coaxes young children into being readers and writers. What might such an environment look like? It should contain two key centers: (1) a library center with lots of books and an environment that encourages reading and (2) a writing center that contains materials and resources for writing. In addition to these core literacy centers, teachers should put materials to support children's reading and writing explorations in every area in the classroom.

The Library Center

Did you know that in many early childhood classrooms, books are not present in the quantity, quality, or variety that young children deserve and need to support their learning? In fact, some early childhood classrooms do not even have a library center.

Take a look at Figure 4. This is the kind of well-designed library center that every young learner needs and deserves. Five or six children can fit into this area. Remember, the goal is to create a space that is snug but not cramped. Here, small groups of children can gather to read, write, talk, and listen. Note that the center is labeled, and there is a picture next to the sign showing appropriate center behavior to help the children read the label. Writing tools and blank booklets enable children to record their own stories. With a bit of imagination and planning, the library center can become one of the most inviting areas of the classroom.

• • • • • • • • • • • • • •

Strategies in Use: Reading Tubs

In St. Michael's Day Nursery, each classroom has a brightly colored, painted claw-foot tub filled with pillows. The tubs were gifts of a building demolition contractor. He and a work crew delivered them to the designated spot in each classroom. Two local AmeriCorps VISTA members, as a part of their service commitment, painted the tubs—one red, one blue, one green, one yellow. Colorful pillows from rummage sales, thrift stores, and homes fill the bottom of each tub. One group of children insisted that all the pillows be blue, like water.

Three rules apply to the reading tubs. These rules are posted above each tub, with picture support.

1. Only two children in the tub at one time.

2. Shoes off.

3. Read.

• • • • • • • • • • • • • •

Open-faced and traditional bookshelves provide children with easy access to books. The books on the traditional bookshelf are shelved with their spines out. These types of shelves have the advantage of being able to store lots of books. The open-faced bookshelf does not hold many books, but it allows the children to see each book's cover. Children will choose more books from the open-faced bookshelf than from the traditional bookshelf.

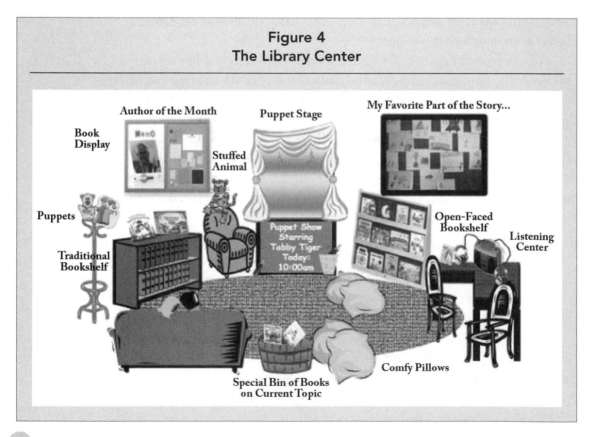

Figure 4
The Library Center

Researchers found that when both types of shelves were used, kindergartners chose more than 90% of their books from open-faced shelves (Fractor, Woodruff, Martinez, & Teale, 1993). Some teachers put all the books about the current topic of study into a special bin. During Time to Read and Activity Time, the children are free to select books from this special collection as well as books from the bookshelves.

If an open-faced bookshelf is too expensive for a center's budget, Gambrell (2000) suggests teachers make a book rail. A book rail accomplishes the same function as an open-faced bookshelf—it displays books so that children can see the covers. The only difference is that, instead of being free-standing, it is attached to a wall. Here is how Gambrell suggests that teachers make their own book rail:

1. Go to a home repair store.
2. Purchase a piece of aluminum drain gutter.
3. Back in the classroom, rest the gutter against the wall (or attach it to the wall at eye level, if this is permitted) and put books facing out into the slot.

Goal: To catch readers!

Numerous props, such as puppets, stuffed animals, and a flannel board with storybook characters are available for the children's use. Children might decide to read a book to a teddy bear or retell a story using hand puppets or flannel board characters, or they might collect three bears and retell the story of the three little bears with friends.

Book-related displays including an author bulletin board attract children to the center. Inexpensive posters to brighten the center and encourage reading can be obtained from the Children's Book Council and the American Library Association. Also, the exhibit halls at regional and national teacher and library conferences are excellent sources for free children's book posters.

The better the design of the library center, the more the children use it. Does the library center in the preschool classroom you know best look like Figure 4? What about the books in the library center? What materials are needed to support children's literacy learning? If there are 15 children in a preschool classroom, how many books should be in the library center? Morrow (2005) recommends that a classroom library should contain 5 to 8 books per child. That means that a classroom with 15 children needs 75 to 120 books. Building a collection of this size need not be expensive.

Building a Classroom Library.   The following are some inexpensive ways to build a classroom library:

- Invite a local club to adopt your classroom. Ask the club to contact members for picture books and children's magazine donations.
- Visit area flea markets, rummage sales, and thrift stores. Get to know the clerks. Perhaps they'll call when picture books are donated.
- Make friends with your local public library's children's librarian. Arrange to borrow as many books as possible each month. Here you will find a ready source of books linked to the topic being studied in the classroom. If the public library is within walking distance, arrange to take the children to the library to introduce them to the wonders available there.
- Organize a fundraiser to purchase books for the classroom.
- Invite parents to give a book to the classroom in honor of their child's birthday.
- Join a paperback book club and use the bonus points to purchase books.

Some of the 75 to 120 books in the classroom library center need to remain in the center for the entire year. These are the core books that children continuously read and reread. These are the books whose titles the children shout when asked, "What would you like me to read to you today?" Other books will rotate in and out of the center. Often, these books are linked with the topic the children are studying. Studying transportation? Gather books about cars, trucks, taxis, and airplanes from your local library. Studying food? The library center needs both fiction and informational books on different foods.

Selecting Books for the Classroom Library.   What kinds of books belong in a preschool classroom library? Strive to provide quality literature on a variety of topics. Table 1 offers a few recommendations, including longstanding favorites and some newer titles.

Young children are very curious about how their world works. Therefore, including nonfiction books in the library center is critical. Yet Duke's (2000) study of young children's classrooms found very few informational books. What kinds of books are in the preschool classroom you know best? How many books of each kind are available for the children's

Table 1
List of Recommended Books for the Classroom Library

- Traditional stories such as *Goldilocks and the Three Bears* (Aylesworth, 2003) and *Just a Minute: A Trickster Tale and Counting Book* (Morales, 2003)
- Picture books with rich language, varied sentence structure, and sophisticated vocabulary, such as *My Family Plays Music* (Cox, 2003), *My Name Is Yoon* (Recorvits, 2003), and *My Friend Rabbit* (Rohmann, 2002)
- Classic storybooks by authors such as Tomie dePaola, Eric Carle, Paul Galdone, Tana Hoban, Ezra Jack Keats, Leo Lionni, and Robert McCloskey
- Poetry including *Pío Peep! Traditional Spanish Nursery Rhymes* (Ada & Campoy, 2003), *Honey, I Love and Other Love Poems* (Greenfield, 1978), *Up the Hill and Down* (Smith, 2003), *Best Mother Goose Ever!* (Scarry, 1999), and *Will Moses' Mother Goose* (Moses, 2003)
- Alphabet books such as *The Animal ABC* (Baker, 2003), *ABC: A Child's First Alphabet Book* (Jay, 2003), *Chicka Chicka Boom Boom* (Martin & Archambault, 1989), and *Alphabeep: A Zipping, Zooming ABC* (Pearson, 2003)
- Predictable stories such as *Brown Bear, Brown Bear, What Do You See?* (Martin, 1992), *Chicken Soup With Rice* (Sendak, 1962), *Ella Sarah Gets Dressed* (Chodos-Irvine, 2003), *I Kissed the Baby* (Murphy, 2003), and *Hi, Harry* (Waddell, 2003)
- Informational or expository texts such as *Truck* (Crews, 1997), *Tool Book* (Gibbons, 1988), *The Quicksand Book* (dePaola, 1977), *What Do You Do With a Tail Like This?* (Jenkins & Page, 2003), *What Is an Artist?* (Lehn, 2002), and *I Face the Wind* (Cobb, 2003)

use in this classroom? What about children's magazines? These, too, should be found in the library center.

The Writing Center

Some teachers put the writing center in a section of the library center. They put a table, chairs, writing tools, and small blank books in the library center to encourage children to write books. Others set up a writing center adjacent to the library center with lots of different kinds of paper and writing tools for children's use.

In the writing center, teachers can provide models of different types of writing, including invitations, greeting cards, postcards, letters, and thank-you notes, for the children to use as a resource for writing. Another important resource is alphabet strips, laid flat on the table so children can hunt for and copy the letters they need. Often, children will write using their personal script, ignoring the alphabet strip—they are, after all, preschool children. Teachers should also stock the writing center with materials that invite children to write and to play with writing. Consider the following possibilities:

- Assorted paper, such as unlined paper, envelopes, note cards, story paper, paper cut into different shapes, and discarded office paper with one clean side
- An assortment of writing tools such as pencils, markers, crayons, felt-tip pens, and a computer
- Mailboxes for everyone in the class
- Writing folders
- A bulletin board for displaying writing samples and children's writing efforts
- Posters of people engaged in writing
- Wooden or magnetic alphabet letters
- Clipboards

Such enticing materials coax young children into becoming writers. Labeled storage areas enable children to participate in clean-up.

Should computers be included in the writing center? Definitely yes! Some fortunate young children have access to computers at home. The language of computers is a natural part of their vocabulary, and they are accustomed to using computers to support their learning. But all preschoolers need such opportunities. Otherwise, the digital divide will persist and inevitably some children will miss the chance to learn with this valuable resource. A computer in the classroom is a tool, just like a pencil or a book. Put books and writing implements in the classroom, and they become a part of the children's lives. Put computers in the classroom, and the same thing happens.

• • • • • • • • • • • • • •

Strategies in Use: Computers as Tools for Literacy Play

Angie finds 3-year-old Lauren sitting at the keyboard, tapping the computer keys. Cautiously, she asks, "What are you doing, Lauren?" Lauren turns and says, "Checkin' my e-mail."

• • • • • • • • • • • • • •

New software packages appear on the market each year. For some preschool classrooms, computers are an expensive tool. To stretch the budget as far as possible, contact a local business (e.g., a bank or university) to learn about the possibility of securing their "gently used" computers and printers for free. Then, technology funds can be used to purchase the software and Internet access needed to make the computers useful to the children.

Planning for Children's Play

Having books and writing tools in the library center and writing center is not enough. Print and tools to make print need to be placed in every classroom center—dramatic play, art, science, math, and so forth. When reading and writing are part of every activity, young children have many opportunities to learn, practice, and consolidate literacy concepts and skills.

Creating Literacy-Enriched Play Settings

By embedding reading and writing materials into dramatic play centers, teachers provide children with opportunities to do what Bruner (1984) calls "run ups" to literacy. Through their play in these literacy-enriched play settings, children can practice being readers and writers. They get to try on the role of taxi driver, garage worker, doctor, or architect and to use the tools of literacy connected with each role. They provide receipts for rides given or car repairs made. They read the stop signs as they drive their customers to their destination. They read and follow the directions for changing a tire. They write prescriptions. They read magazines while they wait for their doctor's appointment. They make architectural drawings before they build, labeling the parts of the building.

There is a powerful research base that supports the importance of teachers providing children with literacy-enriched play opportunities. Roskos and Christie (2004) studied the literacy-enriched play research and came to three conclusions:

1. Play provides a setting that promotes literacy activity, skills, and strategies.
2. Play serves as a language experience that can build connections between oral and written modes of expression.
3. Play provides opportunities for teachers to teach and children to learn literacy.

So, what might these play environments look like? What should teachers consider as they plan for children's play in literacy-enriched play settings?

The first, key principle is that young children play best at what they know. Therefore, literacy-enriched play settings should reflect real-life literacy situations (Neuman & Roskos, 1992). Teachers can support children in playing what they know—both by establishing play environments that relate to children's life experience and by providing classroom experiences that extend children's knowledge base.

Children come to school knowing something about family life. Common experiences include caring for a baby, shopping for groceries, cooking, and eating meals. Therefore, many preschool teachers set up a home play setting in the dramatic play center. These home play settings can be easily turned into literacy-enriched play environments by adding reading materials typical of a home, such as a telephone directory, books, television guides, newspapers and magazines, advertisements, cookbooks, and coupons, as well as writing materials such as pencils and notepads, sticky notes, stationery and envelopes, and checkbooks. When these materials are available for children's use in their play episodes, they will use them. The materials will nudge them to behave like readers and writers.

Near the housekeeping center, some teachers establish a theme setting based on the topic the children are studying. If space is limited, the housekeeping center can gradually be converted into a theme center, with new play props for each topic of study. For example, when studying food, the theme setting often is a restaurant. When studying transportation, the theme setting might be a garage, a taxi stand, a bus, or an airport terminal. When studying health, the theme setting might be a doctor's office. Because most children have visited a pediatrician's office or health clinic, this is often an effective setting. Many children are fascinated by animals, and a veterinarian's office is another possibility—one that might add a new word to the children's vocabulary. By drawing from children's experiences at home, in school, and in the community, teachers can plan meaningful and productive settings.

In setting up a theme center, it is essential to use furniture and props suggestive of real-world settings. For example, a veterinarian's office might be divided into a waiting area and an examination room. In the waiting area, patients might sit in chairs, while a receptionist sits behind a desk and jots down essential information. Literacy props in this area could include reading material for pet owners and a telephone book, message pad, appointment book, patient folders, and forms and clipboards for the receptionist. Wall signs such as "Exit," "Please Ring Bell for Service," and "The Doctor Is In" enhance the literacy environment.

Surrounding the examination table, literacy props might include a doctor's kit, a scale, and informational books and charts about pets. Given such materials, children will recall their own experiences at the doctor's office and will draw from their observations of adults engaged in medical roles. Because the tools needed by readers and writers are readily available to the children, the children will incorporate them into their play. They will sign the appointment book, fill out the required forms, answer the telephone, and take messages. They will behave like readers and writers, using the language associated with the roles they assume. For additional ideas on literacy materials that might be added to various thematic play settings, see Appendix A.

Such play settings provide children with a supportive context for meaningful, authentic interactions with reading and writing. While children play, they have the opportunity to practice learning about the purposes for print and about the conventions of writing and reading. And as they play, they begin to see reading and writing as something they want to be able to do. Thus, linking literacy and play builds print motivation—positive attitudes toward reading and writing that can have an important role in later literacy learning.

Children's writing during play may not be conventional print. In fact, it probably will not be. See Figure 5 for an example of scribble writing inspired by a supportive play setting.

Figure 5
Children's Writing in Play Settings

"One hamburger, plain, and one hamburger with cheese"

Children come to understand that print has meaning. In the following classroom scene, notice how Kayla uses writing.

• • • • • • • • • • • • • •

Strategies in Use: Writing During Play

The play setting is a restaurant. Kayla, the waitress with an order pad and pencil in hand, approaches a table of customers with the questions, "What do ya want? 'Paghetti? Hamburger?" After considerable negotiating about what really is available from the menu and several conversations with the cook, the customers decide on spaghetti, one with meatballs and one without meatballs. Kayla writes the order, using scribblelike script. She tears the order from the pad and hands it to the cook, saying, "Two orders of 'paghetti, one with meatballs and one with none." The cook looks at the order and asks, "What did you write?" Kayla responds, "'Paghetti with meatballs and 'paghetti with none! And hurry up! They are hungry!" The cook gets busy banging pots and cooking.

• • • • • • • • • • • • • •

What does Kayla show us she knows? She demonstrated her awareness of the practical functions of print. To remember an order, she needed to write it down. She also knows that print has meaning—and she knows what her print means.

Signs such as "Please Wait to Be Seated" or "No Customers in the Kitchen" encourage children to ask, "What does that say?" They quickly understand that this print also has meaning—and they use that knowledge to control their peers' behavior. "You can't go in the kitchen. Only me!" Also, repeated exposure to print props gives children opportunities to recognize sight words. They begin to read *No*, *Exit*, *Open*, and *Closed*.

• • • • • • • • • • • • • •

Strategies in Use: Understanding That Print Has Meaning

Jasmine and Tiki are playing together in the shoe store dramatic play center. When any other child approaches, one of them runs to the "Closed" sign and says, "What does this say? Closed. We'll tell you when we are open. You can't come in 'til then."

• • • • • • • • • • • • • •

Some children begin to recognize letters through their repeated exposure to print during play. For example, they begin to recognize *O* because it is the first letter in *Open*. Other children might begin to learn about sound–symbol relationships. For example, if *pizza*, *pepperoni*, and *Pepsi* are on the menu in the restaurant play center, children may begin to discover that all these words start with the same sound and that this sound is represented by the letter *p*.

Enriching Other Centers With Literacy

Of course, this literacy-enrichment strategy is not restricted to the literacy centers. If pencils and markers are placed in the art center, children will have opportunities to write their names on creations. With some guidance from the teacher, they also will begin to write signs (e.g., "Ples dnt tch") to protect art projects in progress. If markers and sign-making materials are placed in the block center, children will make safety signs to go along with their constructions. When pencils and notepads are available in the science center, children can jot down notes and observations. They can record when the fish have been fed or note how many baby fish are still alive.

Putting reading and writing materials in every center not only provides children with the opportunity to handle books, paper, and writing tools, but it also encourages them to use the vocabulary and sentence structures associated with each play setting. Bruner (1983) has noted that the most complex forms of language appear first in children's play activity. Possessing rich language skills is critical to children's later success as readers.

> The most complex forms of language appear first in children's play.

Teacher Involvement in Play

It seems difficult to argue that writing materials and print are not important features of quality dramatic play centers. But still there is something missing—the teacher. With teacher involvement, children learn more about reading and writing than when they play alone or solely with other children. Enz and Christie (1997) describe three important roles that teachers can assume in children's play; each role is important to children's learning.

First, teachers can be stage managers. As stage managers, they gather materials, make props, organize the play area, and talk with the children about how they might play in the setting.

Second, teachers can also be coplayers. As coplayers, they join in the children's play and assume a minor role appropriate to the setting. For example, in a restaurant play setting, they might be customers. In this role, they might ask about the items on the menu, ask about paying with a credit card or with a check, help other customers place their orders, ask about a particular sign, and so forth. Through their behavior, they can model reading and writing behaviors associated with the role, like writing a check.

Finally, teachers can be play leaders. As play leaders, teachers take steps to enrich and extend the play episodes. They introduce conflict into the play. For example, in a restaurant play setting as the customer, a teacher might order something that is not on the menu. When the child says that the requested food is not on the menu, the teacher might ask, "Isn't there anything you can do?" This creates a problem for the children to solve and enriches the play episode. If the children have no suggestions, the teacher might ask, "Could you go to the grocery store to get the ingredients?" If the children agree, then the teacher might question the children's ability to remember everything that is needed by asking, "Is there anything that you could do to help you remember?" Perhaps the children will consider writing a grocery list.

Teachers likely will play each of these roles regularly. The key is to watch the children at play and to choose the role that best fits the children's ongoing play episode.

Evaluating the Classroom Environment and Teacher–Child Interactions

Creating a quality place for children to play and learn requires teachers to carefully plan the classroom environment. When you look at a preschool classroom, ask yourself the following questions:

- Has the large classroom space been divided into small, well-defined areas?

- Was the furniture arranged to encourage the children to interact with each other?

- Are related centers near each other?

- Is each learning center labeled with a sign? Are the signs displayed at children's eye level? Can the children understand the signs?

- Are the storage places for materials labeled?

- Is there functional or environmental print in each center?

- Is there a library center with a generous selection of books? Are the books displayed on both open-faced and traditional bookshelves?

- Is there a writing center that offers an assortment of appealing writing materials with and on which children can write for various purposes?

- Does the dramatic play center contain theme-related reading and writing materials from the world outside the classroom?

- Do the play settings build on the children's background knowledge?

- Does the teacher enter the play settings to play with the children?

If you can answer yes to each of these questions, you know that you are observing a carefully planned, literacy-rich preschool learning environment.

Take a careful look at the list of questions. All but one of the questions focuses on the *physical* environment of the classroom. What's missing are questions about teacher–child interactions. As Neuman and Roskos discovered in their review of the literature, a growing number of researchers have discovered the importance of how teachers interact with children on the children's academic and language development. So how might information on this important element of a literacy-rich preschool learning environment be gathered? An often-used tool was developed by Pianta, La Paro, and Hamre (2008). This observational instrument, called the Classroom Assessment Scoring System (CLASS), measures 10 aspects of teaching. An observer watches the teacher interacting with the children, and the children interacting with each other, and asks questions such as the following:

- Is the teacher connecting with the children, showing respect and enjoyment?

- Are the teacher or the children showing anger? Is the teacher yelling or threatening the children?

- Does the teacher seem to anticipate problems? When a problem occurs, does the teacher address it effectively and in a timely manner? When children need support, do they appear comfortable seeking help?

- Does the teacher follow the children's lead, varying from the lesson plan to follow the children's interests? Does the teacher give the children choices and freedom to move? Does the teacher encourage the children to talk?

- Has the teacher set clear expectations for the children's behavior, and does the teacher use effective methods to prevent or redirect misbehavior?

- Does the teacher make effective use of the instructional time available (e.g., transitions are brief, materials are prepared, children seem to know what to do)?

- Is the teacher actively involved with the children, and are the children actively involved in the activities and lessons? Do the children have many hands-on opportunities?

- Does the teacher ask *why* and *how* questions and provide opportunities for the children to generate their own ideas? Does the teacher link concepts and activities together, building on the children's prior knowledge and previous learning?

- Are there frequent back-and-forth exchanges between the teacher and the children? Does the teacher ask the children to explain their thinking? Does the teacher expand on what the children know, adding new information? Does the teacher offer recognition and encouragement of the children's efforts?

- Does the teacher ask open-ended questions and repeat and expand on the children's responses? Is there lots of conversation in the classroom, between teachers and children and between children and children? Does the teacher use self or parallel talk to describe his or her own actions or the children's actions?

To use the CLASS correctly requires special training. Trainers are working with principals and center directors to help them identify teachers' strengths and weaknesses. Armed with this information, they can plan professional development linked to the teachers' needs. Trainers also are working with teachers across the country to help them think about and improve their interactions with children in their print-rich classroom environment. When teachers and children interact in quality ways in a print-rich classroom environment, children's learning is enhanced.

In this chapter, we discussed and then provided two sets of questions to guide your thinking about how to design a classroom environment that will support children's learning: (1) 11 questions about the physical environment and (2) 10 questions from the CLASS instrument that assess the quality of teacher–child interactions. If you are currently teaching, use these questions to assess the quality of your classroom's physical environment and to reflect on your interactions with your young students. If you are not yet teaching, visit a preschool classroom and use the questions to help you better understand what you see. As you reflect or observe, make a list of the strengths and suggestions for changes to the physical environment and teacher–child interactions.

CHAPTER 3

Planning the Daily Schedule

Reading, writing, and talking are activities that should be incorporated into every part of the preschool schedule every day. Teachers can accomplish this by arranging their daily schedules so that preschoolers are provided with time to investigate on their own during center time, as well as time in small groups with their peers and teachers, and time in a whole group. Each grouping arrangement has its advantages. Whole-group instruction is time efficient: the teacher can deliver instruction to the entire class at one time. Small-group instruction takes more time because instruction is only being delivered to part of the class. However, this instruction can be targeted to the instructional needs of those specific children. Center time activities provide children with opportunities to practice skills. In addition, children get experience with working independently and with peers, promoting self-regulation and the skills needed for collaborative learning.

During whole-group times, the teacher engages all the children in thinking, talking, reading, and writing about ideas related to the topic under study. The teacher reads aloud, tells stories, engages the children in singing songs or reciting poems, presents new materials, and leads the children in brief discussions. During small-group times, the teacher and assistant teacher (and perhaps a parent volunteer) meet with groups of 4–10 children. This is the ideal setting for interactive shared reading, shared writings, brief instructional lessons, and rich discussions. Because of the small-group size, all children get opportunities to participate and be actively engaged in activities. Small groups are ideal settings for younger, less mature children and for those with behavioral issues. In center time, the children move from one literacy-enriched setting to another, exploring the provided materials independently and with peers. During center time, children have an opportunity to practice and consolidated skills that are taught in whole- and small-group instruction. For example, if children are learning about transportation, centers can provide them with activities that encourage them to use transportation-related vocabulary and learn more about the topic (e.g., reading new books about motor vehicles). Language and literacy activities can also be easily woven into transition activities, taking advantage of time that may otherwise be wasted.

Although there is a need for flexibility in the daily schedule so that children are allowed to pursue their interests without interruption, young children also need predictability. Children thrive when they know that the whole-group meeting is followed by center time, that center time is followed by snack time, that snack is followed by small groups, etc.

What might a daily schedule that meets these criteria look like? Tables 2 and 3 provide examples of two preschool schedules, one for a half-day program and the other for a full-day program.

Must teachers follow a prescribed schedule every day? Wien and Kirby-Smith (1998) say no. They suggest that teachers establish a predictable order for daily events; however, teachers should also allow the children to dictate the timing of changes in activities. Wein and Kirby-Smith believe that while children need predictability and structure, they do not necessarily need a schedule determined by the clock. If the children are deeply engaged in investigations during center time, what is wrong with extending their play another 5–10 minutes? On the other hand, if the children seem

Table 2
A Sample Half-Day Schedule

Time	Activity
8:00–8:30	Children arrive, sign in, use library center materials while waiting for group time to begin
8:30–9:00	Whole-group morning gathering, morning messages, discussion of the topic being studied, overview of the day
9:00–10:00	Activity time in literacy-enriched play settings; teacher works with small groups of children on literacy activities suited to their needs
10:00–10:20	Clean-up and snack
10:20–10:45	Shared storybook reading (done in small groups led by teacher and assistant teacher)
10:45–11:15	Outdoor play
11:15–11:45	Whole-group: Songs, poems, movement
11:45–12:00	Review of the day and preparation for going home

Table 3
A Sample Full-Day Schedule

Time	Activity
8:00–8:30	Children arrive, sign in, use library center materials while waiting for group time to begin
8:30–9:00	Whole-group morning gathering, morning messages, discussion of the topic being studied, overview of the day
9:00–10:00	Activity time in literacy-enriched play settings; teacher works with small groups of children on literacy activities suited to their needs
10:00–10:20	Clean-up and snack
10:20–10:45	Shared storybook reading in small groups (teacher and assistant teacher)
10:45–11:15	Outdoor play
11:15–11:45	Whole-group: Songs, poems, movement
11:45–12:15	Lunch
12:15–12:40	Storybook reading in small groups
12:40–1:40	Outdoor play
1:40–2:10	Activity time in literacy-enriched settings; teacher works with small groups on math- and science-related activities
2:10–2:40	Whole-group circle time that focuses on summarizing the day's activities, predicts tomorrow's activities, and reviews stories read in group times
2:40–3:00	Review of the day and preparation for going home

disengaged—if they are wandering the classroom and struggling with one another, what is wrong with shortening their center activities by a few minutes? It's the predictable sequence, rhythm, and structure of the day that are important.

Whole-Group Time

Often referred to as "circle time," many preschool teachers schedule a whole-group session at the very beginning of the day and another at the end of the day. During these times, the children and their teacher come together, typically in a carpeted area of the classroom. During the first group time of the day, teachers usually take attendance, make announcements, check the date on the calendar, report on the news of the day, and discuss plans for the day. Other whole-group sessions are used for the teacher to read literature aloud, for singing songs, for brief lessons on skills that most children need to learn, and for bringing closure to the day.

Whole-group instruction is efficient because the teacher can provide instruction to the entire class at the same time. It also builds a sense of classroom community, giving children common experiences that bond them together into a learning community. However, to meet the developmental characteristics of 3- and 4-year-old children, whole-group times should be fast-paced, brief in duration, and engaging. Thirty minutes is usually the maximum length for an effective whole-group session with 4-year-olds. Three-year-olds and less mature 4-year-olds do best with 20-minute sessions. Some teachers schedule 30-minute whole-group sessions, but arrange for the assistant teacher to pull out younger or less mature children after about 15 to 20 minutes. These children are then given small-group instruction, while the rest of the class finishes up the whole-group time.

> To meet the developmental characteristics of 3- and 4-year-old children, whole-group times should be fast-paced, brief in duration, and engaging.

Of course, these recommendations are only approximate, and the optimal length of whole-group sessions is also influenced by content. If children are very interested and engaged in a whole-group lesson, longer time periods are appropriate. Children's attention spans are remarkably long when they are engaged in an activity of interest to them! On the other hand, Neuman and Roskos (2005) describe a classroom situation in which preschool children had to endure a 45-minute circle time in which each child in the class had to come up to the alphabet frieze and point out the first two letters in their name, compare all the letters in the names of the days of the week, and then count up to 30. The children quickly became disengaged and listless. This was caused by a combination of rote, uninteresting skill-and-drill content and too much time. Such lengthy bouts of whole-group teaching are not recommended, as they are counterproductive and almost always lead to behavior problems.

Center Time

Preschool and kindergarten classrooms are commonly divided into activity areas, or learning centers, with each area having its own particular set of materials and activities. In center-based classrooms, children interact with focused sets of materials and help each other build their own knowledge and skills. The teacher's role is to set up the environment, observe as children interact with the materials, supply help and guidance when needed, and occasionally introduce new activities for each center. If centers are set up properly and if an effective management system is established, the classroom environment does much of the "teaching"!

Effective centers are stocked with materials that allow children to learn through exploration and experimentation. The following are examples of common classroom learning centers and some of their materials (Johnson, Christie, & Wardle, 2005):

> If centers are set up properly and if an effective management system is established, the classroom environment does much of the "teaching"!

- Library center—books, magazines, bookshelves, sofa or upholstered chair, rug, and book-related displays (see Chapter 3)

- Writing center—pencils, markers, paper, blank books, alphabet chart, letter stencils, dictionaries, writing folders, individual journals, mailboxes, chalk and chalkboards, and computers (see Chapter 3)

- Dramatic play center—props and furniture that suggest specific settings that are familiar to children, such as a home, grocery store, restaurant, post office, or veterinary hospital (theme-related literacy props should also be included; see Appendix A)

- Block center—unit blocks, large hollow blocks, small replicas of vehicles, people and animals, books on construction, supplies for making signs

- Table toy centers—puzzles, pegboards, dominoes, games, and math manipulatives

- Art center—paints, easels, brushes, scissors, glue, wall paper books, small pieces of wood, paper, felt pens, crayons, clay, print pads and stencils, yarn and cloth samples, and old magazines

- Music center—CD player, MP3 player, rhythm instruments, autoharp, cassettes, and song books

- Science center—class pets, aquarium, objects to sort and feel (e.g., shells, seeds, stones), magnifying glass, balance scale, seeds to grow, ant farm, books about science, water table, sand box, and "found objects" display

- Math center—math manipulatives (cubes, beads), counting frames, math games and puzzles, counting books

Typically, the teacher arouses the children's curiosity or directs their focus during the whole-group meetings. During center time, the children can act on their interests. During these times, the children might move freely about the classroom, selecting the area or center of interest to them. They might write in the writing center, read books in the cozy corner library, build structures in the block or construction center, or investigate and record their observations in the science center. It is important for teachers to both provide children with time to engage in activities of their choice and to plan the use of their time.

Centers offer an ideal opportunity for children to practice and perfect literacy skills. For example, if the teacher has read the Big Book, *Tabby Tiger's Taxi*, to children during whole-group time, children can extend their knowledge of taxies and transportation-related concepts and vocabulary during center time. Children playing in the taxi-theme dramatic play center can hail taxies, drive to various destinations, pay their fares, and receive receipts from the driver. The children also can "read" maps and "drive" cars along pretend roads in the block center. In the writing center, they can make license plates and signs for use in the taxi play center. They can read books on transportation in the library center.

During these free-choice times, the children might work with a small group of peers to answer questions of shared interest. In other instances, groups might form spontaneously; those five children who are interested in playing in the dramatic play area come together for play and stay until they are tired of playing in the center.

It is important for teachers to engage in learning with their children during these free-choice times. This is not the time for teachers to complete administrative tasks. It is the time to read a book with a child or two, take a child's dictation, happen upon a child at just the moment when she or he needs instruction, or to play with the children in the dramatic play area.

Center periods are typically 40–60 minutes in length. Why the long block of time for activity time and the shorter block of time for whole-group time? Young children need a generous uninterrupted block of time for play. It takes considerable time for them to plan their play with their peers, to negotiate roles with each other, and to carry out their play ideas. Children generally require from 30 minutes to an hour to develop and act out a single play scenario (Christie & Wardle, 1992). The best play scenarios evolve over several days, with children resuming and extending their play each day.

Small-Group Time

Increasingly, early childhood teachers are recognizing the need to pull small groups of children together for explicit instruction on the language and literacy skills. Small groups enable all children to actively engage in an activity and have a chance to talk. The smaller the group, the more each child gets to participate. In addition, small groups enable teachers to focus lessons on skills that specific children need to learn. Whole-group instruction, on the other hand, is usually a compromise, teaching skills that many, but not all of the children need.

> Small groups enable all children to actively engage in an activity and have a chance to talk.

According to McGee (2007), preschool teachers typically organize small groups in two ways: (1) having a separate small-group instruction period in which the class is split into groups, with the teacher working with one group and the assistant teacher working with another, and (2) embedding small-group instruction in center time, pulling out a small number of children for intensive instruction while the rest of the class works and plays in centers.

In an example of the "splitting up" strategy, teachers in the Miami/Dade County Early Learning Coalition Early Reading First project in Florida, USA, divided their children into three groups for small-group instruction. For 30 minutes each day, the children rotated among the three literacy activities (spending 10 minutes in each small-group activity). The classroom teacher engaged in a dialogic reading activity with six children; the classroom assistant engaged in a print awareness activity with another group of six children; and a third group of children played independently with literacy-related materials. Every 10 minutes, the children moved to a new activity. In this way, the teachers were able to work with a small group of children explicitly teaching using SBRR-supported strategies. Some days the children with similar literacy needs were grouped together. Other days, the teacher intentionally created small groups of children with differing literacy needs.

The Mohave Desert Early Literacy Coalition Early Reading First project in Bullhead City, Arizona, USA, modified the entire daily schedule to split preschool classes into smaller groups. Each class was divided into two groups based on the children's language and literacy abilities. All children attended the morning session, Monday through Friday. During the afternoon session, half of the children in each class attended afternoon sessions on Mondays and Wednesday, and half attended on Tuesdays and Thursdays. This split schedule allowed afternoon "whole-group" instruction to be delivered to groups of approximately 10 children, increasing participation and interaction opportunities. This split schedule also allowed the teacher and assistant to divide children into even smaller groups of four to five children for instruction that targets each group's specific needs, as identified by continuous progress monitoring with curriculum-based measures.

The other common grouping strategy is for the teacher to pull a very small group of 2 to 5 children aside during center time for more intensive instruction. This "concentrated" instruction is often referred to as Tier 2 instruction as part of Response to Intervention (RTI), and it is intended for children who are not responding well to regular Tier 1 curriculum. (See Figure 6 for more information on RTI and a Tier 2 supplementary vocabulary instructional strategy known as Word Play Time.) Because this very small-group instruction occurs during center time, it preempts the teacher's ability to interact with children while they engage in center activities. McGee (2005) recommends that teachers only teach one such group per day. As she points out, "The conversations that you have with children as they play in centers are important for children's language development, and you don't want to lose those opportunities" (p. 125).

Figure 6
Word Play Time (WPT)—Tier 2 Vocabulary Instruction for At-Risk Preschoolers

Preschool teachers and speech/language specialists in Lorain, Ohio, USA, work together to help at-risk preschoolers learn the vocabulary they need for school readiness. They are implementing WPT as Tier 2 supplementary vocabulary instruction for those preschoolers who need more opportunity to learn new words.

What Is It?

WPT is a "standard treatment protocol" approach in an RTI model of special education services (Fuchs & Fuchs, 2006). This means it offers the *same instructional treatment for different children* at risk in vocabulary. WPT uses a research-backed instructional protocol for a fixed amount of time with small groups of children. It is organized around a Say-Tell-Do-Play structure for teaching new words in the context of a Read Aloud. Here's the WPT protocol.

(continued)

Figure 6 *(continued)*

Word Play Time
Say-Tell-Do-Play Protocol

Read Aloud: _____   Date: _____

Target Words: _____   Photos: Yes   No

Objects: Yes   No

Phase	Step	Protocol	Teaching Actions
Before Reading	1	I Say	T says target word with photo or object
	2	You Say	T asks children to say target word
	3	I Tell	T tells meaning of target word with photo or object
	4	You Tell	T asks children to *turn-n-tell* a friend
	5	*Repeat for each word	
During Reading	6	I Say and Tell	T says and tells target words as needed
	7	You Say and Tell	T asks children to say and turn-n-tell
	8	I Do	T uses action to help define new word
	9	You Do	T asks children to repeat action
After Reading	10	Let's Play	T invites children to play
			T encourages use of target words in play

How Does It Work?

WPT is supplementary instruction that takes place in a small-group setting, generally during center time in the preschool day. It is organized around theme-related read-aloud books. Two times each week for about 20–30 minutes each time, the teacher or a specialist uses the protocol to teach 10 vocabulary words from either one or two different read-alouds to two or three children. Five words are taught in each session. At the end of each week, the children respond to two prompts on a curriculum-based measure to monitor their word learning. Prompt 1 asks each child to identify target words: "We are going to look at these pictures. Show me the _____." Prompt two asks each child to produce target words: "Tell me the name of the picture I point to." Steady progress over a 6–8-week period indicates that the child is responsive to the vocabulary instruction and does not need more intensive intervention.

WPT uses these steps:

> Step 1: Screen for children at-risk in vocabulary knowledge.
> Step 2: Implement WPT on a regular schedule.
> Step 3: Monitor children's progress weekly using brief prompts.
> Step 4: Determine criterion for adequate improvement (e.g., 80%).
> Step 5: Decide next steps for those who do not respond.

(continued)

Figure 6 (continued)

This is a brief WPT plan for the read-aloud book *Swimmy* by Leo Lionni.

Book	SAY	TELL (Definition)	DO (Action)	PLAY
Swimmy Leo Lionni	sea	A large body of water that is larger than a pond.	Spread out your arms	Reenact/retell the story with stick puppets. Teacher holds backdrop of the sea.
	fish	An animal that lives in water	Make swimming motions	
	escaped	To get away from a place where you don't want to be.	Move feet fast	
	lobster	A fish with claws and a hard body	Make hands look like Claws	
	giant	Large in size (or the name of a very large person)	Lift shoulders and arms.	

Where Do the Target Words Come From?

There are three sources of target words for vocabulary instruction in WPT.

1. Basic words are related to basic concepts of location, position, and direction. Sample words are *up, in, near, far.*
2. Root words are words with a single meaning. *Fish, hope,* and *drop* are examples of root words. The **Living Word Vocabulary** provides an excellent source of root words (Dale & O'Rourke, 1981; see also Biemiller & Slonim, 2001; Dolch, 1948).
3. Rare words are specialized words related to disciplinary knowledge. Words like *habitat, stethoscope,* and *subtract* are specialized vocabulary words.

For each read-aloud book used in WPT, the Lorain teachers and speech/language specialists select a mix of 10 words that represent basic words, root words, and rare words. They currently have a collection of 250 vocabulary words taught in WPT.

Field studies show that WPT helps at-risk children in vocabulary make steady progress in acquiring new words they need for school readiness (Roskos, 2008; Roskos et al., 2008). They make significant gains in identifying and producing new words. And they learn a variety of words that lay solid foundations for school learning.

Note. Provided by Kathleen Roskos.

Transitions

Transitions are the times during the daily schedule when children move from one activity to another. These transition times commonly include arriving at the beginning of the day; moving between whole-group, small-group, and center activities; preparing for outdoor play, meals, and nap time; and getting ready to go home (Hemmeter, Ostrosky, Artman, & Kinder, 2008). There are several reasons why teachers should pay close attention to these transition periods. First, research has shown the preschoolers typically spend as much as 20%–35% of their time in these transitions (Wilder, Chen, Atwell, Pritchard, & Weinstein, 2006), so transitions take up a significant portion of the daily schedule. Second, transitions often lead to challenging behaviors, particularly if transitions are too numerous, too lengthy, or inadequately planned (Hemmeter et al., 2008).

Ostrosky, Jung, and Hemmeter (2008) recommend the following strategies to support smooth transitions:

- Provide verbal ("Five minutes until clean-up") and nonverbal (ringing a bell) reminders before transitions start.
- Allow children to move individually from one area to another without having to wait for the whole group to get ready (after children have finished their snack, they can get a library book and read it while waiting for small group instruction to start).
- Provide positive feedback when children follow transition routines.
- Teach peers to help children who have a difficult time with transitions (e.g., transition buddies).

We also recommend making transition activities educational and engaging. Transitions can provide a perfect opportunity for children to practice language and literacy skills. The Arizona Centers of Excellence in Early Education project in San Luis, Arizona, USA, suggests having children say a "password" when entering the classroom after outdoor play (see ace3.asu.edu). This password can be a theme-related vocabulary word on a poster or picture/word card. During a transportation unit, the passwords were the names of different kinds of motor vehicles. During a construction unit, the passwords were the names of tools. In another example, teachers could have each child quickly point to a letter on the Word Wall when transitioning from large group to center activities.

These activities are done at a brisk pace so that no child needs to wait for more than two or three minutes to get his or her turn. Of course, if children have difficulty doing the task, this presents an excellent opportunity for some teacher scaffolding.

Pulling It All Together: The Daily Schedule

Effective preschool teachers embed reading, writing, talking, and listening into every component of the daily schedule. They provide children with long blocks of time for individual and small-group activities and shorter blocks of time for whole-group gatherings. Effective teachers consider the children's level of engagement as they guide the day's activities. They move on to something new when the children are not working well together and allow extra time for exploration when something captures their interest.

PROFESSIONAL DEVELOPMENT FOR PRE- AND INSERVICE TEACHERS

This chapter discusses planning the daily preschool schedule. We recommend that this schedule include whole-group, small-group, and center times connected by efficient transitions. The following principles enable preschool teachers to create a daily schedule that is sensitive to young children's learning and developmental needs:

- Quiet times should be balanced with noisier times, and sitting and listening time should be balanced with movement time.
- Large blocks of time for individual and small-group investigations should be balanced with shorter amounts of time for whole-group activities.
- Plan transitions that are brief, educational, and engaging.

If you are currently teaching, rate how your own daily schedule meets each of these criteria. If you are not yet teaching, visit a nearby preschool and evaluate its daily schedule with these criteria. If the schedule does not fully meet a criterion, decide how the schedule could be altered and improved so that each criterion can be met.

CHAPTER 4

Reading Aloud: Sharing Books With Young Children

Emergent literacy researchers said it. Scientifically based reading researchers are saying it. There is one activity that is *the* most important activity for parents and preschool teachers to do to support young children's development of the skills required to learn to read. Proponents of both emergent literacy and scientifically based early literacy instruction agree that parents and preschool teachers must read aloud to and with children on a regular basis. Here is how Adams (1990), who studied decades of research, summed up her findings: "The single most important activity for building the knowledge and skills eventually required for reading appears to be reading aloud to children" (p. 46).

Given the importance of this activity, it is fitting for us to dedicate a chapter to the discussion of *how* to share books with young children. We begin by briefly highlighting what research tells us about *why* teachers should read aloud to children. Then, we consider the issues of quantity and quality of adults' storybook reading. Finally, we describe research-based strategies that preschool teachers should use with their children to maximize the value of each storybook reading.

What the Research Says

Sharing books with children helps them develop many of the skills that researchers have identified as essential for later reading success—those skills that we identified in Chapter 1. For instance, reading to young children positively effects their language and vocabulary development, both their receptive vocabulary (e.g., Aram, 2006; Beck & McKeown, 2007; Justice, Meier, & Walpole, 2005) and their expressive vocabulary (Arnold, Lonigan, Whitehurst, & Epstein, 1994; Beck & McKeown, 2007). Through listening to books read aloud to them, children are exposed to words beyond those they hear in their everyday conversations with the people in their lives. That is, book language is *decontextualized*. Through listening to stories read aloud to them, children learn words connected to places they have never been, foods they have never eaten, experiences they have yet to have, and so on. They learn descriptive adjectives, like *grumpy*, *fierce*, and *scary*. Through participating in read-alouds, children are exposed to the sound structure and grammar of the language. They hear the book's characters talk in ways that may be different from the structure and grammar used in their home environment. They hear sentences constructed in ways that likely are different from the spoken language they hear. They also learn the pragmatic rules that govern the use of the language (Ezell & Justice, 2005).

In addition, children learn how texts are organized (or acquire a sense of the text's structure) through participating in storybook reading events (Dickinson & Snow, 1987; Duke & Kays, 1998). For example, through exposure to narrative stories, children learn that narratives have characters, characters have problems, the story happens in a particular place or setting, and stories have a beginning, middle, and end—a sequence. Through exposure to expository or informative texts, children learn about other organizing patterns (like compare and contrast, cause and effect, problem and solution). This knowledge aids in their comprehension of the story.

Sharing books with children helps them develop many of the skills that researchers have identified as essential for later reading success.

Further, through storybook reading, children are exposed to the alphabet and the way in which letters and sounds map on to one another in an alphabetic language. This exposure enhances children's alphabet knowledge—both letter naming and letter sounds.

Quantity Versus Quality

It is not just exposure alone—an adult reading a book aloud to listening children—that makes the difference in children's literacy skill development. It is *how* adults read to the children—and *how often*—that is key to children's language and literacy skill development and to their later success as readers.

The How Often

More than 20 years ago, Wells (1985) provided longitudinal evidence of the effects of frequency of book reading on children's later language development. He reported that the frequency with which children between the ages of 1 and 3 were read to was later positively associated with teachers' ratings of these children's oral language development. Educators responded very enthusiastically to this news. More recent researchers, however, have questioned just how important how often is. These researchers (e.g., Bus et al., 1995; Scarborough & Dobrich, 1994) have concluded that frequency of book reading in children's early years alone contributes only about 7%–10% to children's later success as readers. This news sent educators and researchers to work developing and testing ideas on ways to maximize the impact of regular read-alouds on children's language and literacy development.

The How

How teachers read aloud to children is very important (Beauchat, 2008). In the following section, we describe how teachers of young children use research-based strategies to maximize their children's learning of language and early reading skills.

Explicitly Teach Words.   Just reading storybooks with wonderful words *might* result in some children learning the words. Although some young children are "language sponges," soaking up and later trying out the words they hear, for many children, exposure alone is not enough. Some researchers suggest that children will learn vocabulary words if their teachers reread the same books to them (Sénéchal, 1997). Hearing the same words used over and over helps children learn them. Sénéchal, Thomas, and Monker (1995) suggest another strategy: Children will learn new vocabulary words when they are asked to answer questions about the target words. Still other researchers (Beck & McKeown, 2007; Wasik & Bond, 2001) suggest that teachers should expose children to target words before and after reading. Prior to reading a storybook, the teacher might present the children with concrete objects representing the words and a definition. It is essential that the teacher must select target words and that the teacher must intentionally teach the words to the children.

> It is essential that the teacher must select target words and that the teacher must intentionally teach the words to the children.

Nearly every storybook is a treasure trove of many words that likely are not in the children's listening or speaking vocabulary, so which words should be targeted? As we noted in Chapter 1, determining which words to target takes some careful thinking. Which words are central to understanding the story? Which words might be useful to children not only in understanding this story, but also in other contexts? Which words might the children not hear in their everyday conversations that happen around them?

After selecting the words, teachers of young children might use a strategy like the following:

- During the storybook reading, say the word and ask the children to say the word.

- After saying the word, give a quick child-friendly definition. Sometimes ask the children to repeat the child-friendly definition to a friend.

- After reading the storybook, return to some of the keywords and talk about them with the children.

• • • • • • • • • • • • • •

Strategies in Use: Vocabulary-Focused Storybook Reading

Lynn Hamilton selected *I Will Never NOT Ever Eat a Tomato* (Child, 2000) to read to her 3- and 4-year-old Head Start children as a part of the topic they are studying, Healthy Me. The book contains many references to healthy food (e.g., peas, carrots, potatoes, cauliflower, cabbage, bananas, oranges, apples, tomatoes, mushrooms, etc.). Before sharing the story with her children, she pages through the book to select words her children likely would not know—*difficult, fussy, rare, nibble, mashed, gobbling*. After she reads the last line on the first page, "This is difficult because she is a very fussy eater," she pauses and discusses it with her students.

Lynn: *Difficult.* Can you say that word?

Students: *Difficult.*

Lynn: *Difficult* means that this is not going to be easy. It's going to be very hard. [reading] "This is difficult because she is a very fussy eater." *Fussy.* Say that word.

Students: *Fussy.*

Lynn: *Fussy* means that his little sister is very hard to please—she's choosy. She doesn't like a lot of things.

Lynn uses this strategy as she reads the words she preselected for highlighting with the children. Then, she does more after the storybook reading to build her children's vocabulary. She has read the research that suggests that the frequent use of unfamiliar vocabulary words beyond the storybook reading facilitates the development of vocabulary and that when children have the opportunity to interact with objects for which they do not know the word, their vocabulary increases (Wasik & Bond, 2001). After discussing the story with the children, she pulls a grocery bag from behind the Big Book stand and turns to the page with the beautifully illustrated carrots. She points to the words, each written on a picture of a carrot, and reads and discusses each with the students.

Lynn: I [point] don't [point] ever [point] eat [point] [point and pause, giving the children time to "read"] carrots. [From her bag, she produces a bunch of carrots, complete with the carrot tops.] A bunch of what?

Students: [in unison] Carrots!

Lynn: [turning to the pea page] But I don't eat green things. [From her bag, she produces peas in their pods. She opens one to show the children the peas inside.] What are these? [She holds the peas next to the picture of the peas.] Peas grow inside pods. This is the pod and here are the….

Students: Peas!

Lynn: [repeating process with the potato page and the tomato page] Can you guess what our snack will be today? We're going to slice carrots and shuck peas and peel potatoes and dice tomatoes! Yummy! Ms. Monica will help you slice and shuck and peel and dice at the snack table.

LaDona: But I don't like tomatoes!

Lynn: Ah, you are a fussy eater! Maybe you don't want a tomato, but I bet you'll try a moonsquirter—just like Lola did in the book!

• • • • • • • • • • • • • •

Ask Good Questions.   The dialogic reading strategy, developed by the Stony Brook Reading and Language Project, helps adults read to young children in a way that involves the children in the reading process (Whitehurst, 1992). In dialogic reading, the adult helps the child become actively involved with the story by using prompts and by asking different types of questions. Children whose teachers use this method make greater gains on tests of their language development than children of teachers who do not (What Works Clearinghouse, 2006).

The acronym PEER—representing *prompts*, *evaluates*, *expands*, and *repeats*—demonstrates how dialogic reading works, as follows:

P   The adult *prompts* the child to say something about the book.

E   The adult *evaluates* the child's response.

E   The adult *expands* on the child's response by rephrasing and adding information to the child's response.

R   The adult *repeats* the prompt to make sure that the child has learned from the expansion.

To further help adults, the Stony Brook Reading Project developed a list of types of prompts adults might use. The acronym CROWD— representing *completion*; *recall*; *open-ended*; *what, where, when, and how*; and *distancing*—demonstrates the types of prompts, as follows:

C   *Completion prompts*: Leave a blank at the end of the sentence and ask the children to fill it in. Completion prompts help children learn about the structure of language and the concept of rhyme (words that end with the same sound).

R   *Recall prompts*: These kinds of prompts are questions about the story's plot, sequence of events, or characters.

O   *Open-ended prompts*: Prompts like "Tell me about what you see happening in this picture?" "What do you think [the character] might be thinking?" encourage children to attend to details. These questions have no one right answer.

W   *What, where, when, and how question prompts*: These questions have one right answer—and the answer is right in the book. For example, the teacher might point to each of the animals in a book and ask the children to name each one.

D *Distancing prompts*: These kinds of prompts ask the children to relate what was read to events outside the book. Distancing prompts link the book's text and the children's experiences.

Until they become familiar with talking about the story as it unfolds, young children might have difficulty answering the questions their teachers pose. Beauchat (2008) suggests that teachers of young children might begin by using a gradual release of responsibility approach (Pearson & Gallagher, 1983). Teachers begin by thinking aloud to show the children how they are comprehending the story as they read the storybook.

For example, Lynn Hamilton—the teacher whose classroom is discussed in the previous Strategies in Use vignette—might have looked at the cover of *I Will Never NOT Ever Eat a Tomato* and said, "Looking at the picture on this cover, I know that this book is going to be about a boy and a girl. I know that the boy's name is Charlie because it says 'Charlie' on his shirt. The words tell me that one of them, either the boy or the girl, does not like tomatoes. I wonder if it is the boy or the girl who doesn't like tomatoes." As Beauchat (2008) suggests, this teacher's talk shows the children what good readers do before they begin the reading process. Teachers continue this process as they read the book's pages, making predictions and checking the accuracy of their predictions as the story unfolds, asking questions, and making connections. Teachers might engage in this think-aloud procedure during the first week or so of school, gradually involving the children more and more in describing what they see, making predictions, asking questions and so forth. In this supportive, scaffolded way, the children learn how to co-construct the meaning of the story, to comprehend the story, with the teacher.

• • • • • • • • • • • • • • •

Strategies in Use: Dialogic Reading

Lynn reads her students the first page of the story, *I Will Never NOT Ever Eat a Tomato* (Childs, 2000), and discusses the story with her students.

Lynn: Oh-oh! Charlie has a problem. What is Charlie's problem?

Chloe: She won't eat tomatoes.

Lynn: Well, the title told us that someone (on this page, we learned that it was the little girl and that her name is

Lola, didn't we?) didn't like tomatoes. But I'm wondering, is it just tomatoes that she doesn't like? Why might I be thinking that Lola might not like other foods also? [The children seem confused. Lynn reads.] "Sometimes Mom and Dad ask me to give Lola dinner. This is difficult because she is a very...."

Students: Fussy eater.

Lynn: Right! [evaluates the children's response] Lola is a very fussy, choosy eater. [expansion of the children's response] It doesn't say that feeding her dinner will be difficult because she doesn't like tomatoes, does it? It says that she is what kind of eater? [She repeats the prompt to ensure the children's learning.]

Students: Fussy eater.

Lynn: What other kinds of food might Lola not like? [open-ended prompt] I'll write your ideas on the white board so we can see if you were right later. [The children name lettuce, carrots, bananas, applesauce, which they'd just had for breakfast.]

Lynn: So, I wonder what Charlie is going to do to get Lola to eat dinner! Let's read on and see. [She reads the next two pages where Charlie asks Lola if she likes peas, and Lola says that they are "too small and green." She reads the last line on the page.] "One day I played a good trick on her." Uh-oh! So how is Charlie going to get his sister to eat dinner? He's going to play a good _____ on her." [completion prompt]

Students: He is going to trick her.

Lynn follows through with the evaluate, expand, and repeat components of dialogic reading. As she reads the book's other pages, she asks many questions, and she encourages the children to ask questions such as the following:

- How do you think Charlie felt when Lola said all those foods she didn't like? (open-ended question)

- What kind of trick did Charlie play on his sister? (what recall question) Has anyone ever played a food trick on you? (distancing question)

- Did Charlie's trick work? How do you know that it worked? (how question)

- What could Lola be pointing at when she said "Charlie, will you pass me one of those?" and Charlie said, "What, one of those?" (what question, limited open-ended question)

- Why was Charlie surprised that Lola wanted a tomato? (why question)

After the storybook reading, Lynn asks, "So, did Lola really not like tomatoes? Remember that's what the title said, *I Will Never NOT Ever Eat a Tomato*. Did she eat a tomato? How did Charlie make Lola think that peas, carrots, fish sticks, and mash potatoes were really good things to eat?" Through their discussion, the children begin to understand that Charlie's trick was that he called the foods that Lola didn't like by another name. Lynn dismisses the children to center time with the reminder that they will be dicing moonsquirters, shucking green drops, slicing orange twiglets, and peeling cloud fluff.

• • • • • • • • • • • • • •

Explicitly Teach Book and Print Concepts. Morrow (2009, p. 189) and Ezell and Justice (2005, p. 89) outline the following concepts about books and **print knowledge** that young children need to acquire.

1. Books are for reading.
2. A book's name is its title.
3. A book's writer is the author.
4. A book's illustrator is the person who draws the pictures.
5. Books have a front and a back, a top and a bottom.
6. Pages have a top and a bottom.
7. Turn the pages of a book, one by one, properly, from front to back.

8. Pictures on a book's page relate to what the print says, but the print tells the story.

9. Readers begin reading the first line of print on the left and read toward the right.

10. Print shapes are called alphabet letters; each letter has a name and makes a sound (or sometimes more than one sound) when said.

11. Words are made up of letters.

12. Two words have a space between them.

Some children will learn these concepts just by the adults reading many, many books to them. Other children need adults to explicitly reference these concepts during storybook reading. Unfortunately, Justice, with different colleagues (Justice, Bowles, & Skibbe, 2006; Justice & Ezell, 1998, 2000), found that teachers rarely reference print during storybook readings—and that if teachers don't reference print during their storybook reading, children do not focus on the print. These findings led Ezell and Justice (2005) to describe several strategies that teachers might incorporate into their storybook readings to highlight the print. Debbie Helman's reading of *Tabby Tiger, Taxi Driver* to her Head Start children—as illustrated in the next Strategies in Use vignette—demonstrates several of their strategies. Incidentally, when reading to groups of children with the intention of focusing on building children's print concepts, oversized storybooks with enlarged pictures and print (Big Books) are better than regular-sized books; children can see the print.

• • • • • • • • • • • • • •

Strategies in Use: Concepts of Print

Debbie Helman's 4-year-old Head Start children are seated on the carpet in front of the Big Book stand. Today's Big Book storybook reading is *Tabby Tiger, Taxi Driver* (Cowley, 2001). This is the third day that Debbie has read the story to the children. On the first day, she shared the pictures with the children and asked them to predict what the story would be about. On the second day, she read the words and talked with the children about the content of the story; together, they constructed the meaning of the story. Now, she is ready to read the book for the third time, on Day 3. The back of the book is facing the children, and it is turned upside down.

Debbie:	I can hardly wait to see what Tabby Tiger is doing today! [turns toward the book and tries to open it] Something's wrong here! I can't open the book! [The children suggest that she should turn it "to the front." She does, but leaves it upside down.]
Marcus:	No, the other way! [jumps up to fix the book for her]
Debbie:	[reads the title, pointing to each word] That's the name of the book, right? And the author is Joy Cowley. What does the author do?
Students:	[in unison] She writes the words.
Debbie:	And the illustrator is John Nez. What does the illustrator do?
Amir:	Draws the pictures.
Debbie:	You are so smart, all of you! You know that the author writes the [pauses for the children to fill in "words"] and the illustrator [pauses for the children to fill in "draws the pictures"] I'll turn the page to begin reading. I'll start reading right here on this page [points to left page] and then I'll read this page [points to the right page]. I'll read the first word on the first line and then which way will I read? [Samira takes the pointer and follows the line of print to the right.]
Debbie:	Thanks for helping me know where to read, Samira! [She reads the words on pages 2 and 3 of the book, pointing to each word as she reads and making a return sweep at the end of the line. On page 4, she reads the words without pointing.] Did I read this [pointing to the picture] or did I read this [pointing to the words]?
Students:	The words!

Debbie continues reading and talking about the story with the children. The next day, Day 4, Debbie begins the storybook reading event.

Debbie: Asha, I'd like to invite you to do something I've never asked any of you to do before. Could you come up here, take the pointer, and point to the words as we—your friends and me—read the words? [Asha collects the pointer and points to the words as Debbie and the children read. Multi-syllable words are a little bit of a challenge, so Debbie helps with some of the pointing.]

Debbie: [turns to title page] *Tabby Tiger, Taxi Driver* contains lots of upper case *T*s. Look very closely at this page. When you've found an upper case *T*, raise your hand. [Hands shoot up and children come forward to put pieces of highlighter tape on the upper case *T* that they see. When all the *T*s have been found, Debbie turns the page, and the hunt is on for more *T*s. When all have been found, the children count how many upper case *T*s they found in the book.]

On Day 5, Debbie's focus shifts to the number of words and sentences on a page. After the children and she read the book aloud (by now the children know the words in the book), she turns to the first page.

Debbie: How many words are on this page? Before we count them, here's what I want you to do. I've made some tiny pieces of highlighter tape. When I call your name, I want you to come up here and put one of these tiny pieces of highlighter tape right in the space between two words. Let me show you. [She models, and then begins to call children up to put the highlighter tape in the space between two words. Then she writes "page 2" on a piece of chart paper with the title "Which page has the most words?" The children count the number of words, and she writes the number. When all spaces have been marked and all words on each page counted and recorded, she reads the title of the chart paper, "Which page has the most words?"]

Students: Page 16!

Debbie: Which page has the fewest number of words? [The
children decide on pages 7 and 8. There are no
words on these pages. They agree that the page with
the fewest number of "real" words is page 13.]

Over these three days, Debbie focused her children's attention
on the print in the big book. She implicitly addressed concepts 1, 6,
7 above and explicitly taught concepts 2, 3, 4, 5, 8, 9, 10, and 12. The
only print concept she did not address was words are made up of
letters. Next week with a new book, she'll explicitly teach several of
the concepts taught on these three days and focus the children's attention on the letters in words.

• • • • • • • • • • • • • • •

Purposely, Playfully, and Systematically Teach Phonological Awareness.

In Chapter 1, we provided a rich description of phonologi-
cal awareness and described several instructional activities that early childhood teachers might use with their children. Storybooks provide an
important venue for developing phonological awareness skills (often referred to as PA skills).

• • • • • • • • • • • • • •

Strategies in Use: PA-Focused Storybook Reading

Melva Jackson-Williams is reading *Warthogs in the Kitchen: A Sloppy
Counting Book* (Edwards, 1998) to her children. Her lesson plan suggests the following:

First reading: During—Focus on rhyming (e.g., today/away,
mess/guess, how/now, there/bear)

Second reading: After—Children clap words as she reads ("I
want to help. I won't make a mess." page 6;
"Six cracked eggs. How many on the floor?"
page 13)

Third reading: During—Focus on *cooks* and *cupcakes*
("What's the first sound you hear in *cooks*
and *cupcakes*? Can you think of other words
that begin like *cooks* and *cupcakes*?")

• • • • • • • • • • • • • •

Maximizing the Impact of Storybook Reading

Clearly, many aspects of the key language and early reading skills can be built into storybook reading. By engaging in these kinds of activities while reading with children, teachers show children how to make sense of the text and how to construct meaning while listening to or reading books. By prompting and encouraging the children to talk (to ask questions, respond to others' questions, and notice the illustrations and the print), the teacher is helping the children understand how readers construct the meaning of a text as the story or information unfolds. Through these activities, teachers can engage their young learners with book and print concepts and with phonological awareness concepts. Storybook reading is a key component of an early childhood classroom's daily schedule. Early childhood teachers want to read often to children, many different books and the same book more than once, and they need to plan each reading carefully to maximize storybook reading's impact on children's language and early reading development.

PROFESSIONAL DEVELOPMENT FOR PRE- AND INSERVICE TEACHERS

Does your storybook reading sound like Debbie Helman's, Melva Jackson-Williams's, and Lynn Hamilton's? Are you using storybook reading as a context within which to teach vocabulary, phonological awareness, print knowledge, and comprehension? To answer these questions, videotape yourself reading to children. As you watch this storybook reading event, ask yourself the following questions:

- Which vocabulary words did I explicitly teach? Did I say the word, ask the children to repeat the word, provide a child-friendly definition, and ask the children to repeat the child-friendly definition?

- Did I prompt the children to say something about the book? Did I evaluate their responses? Did I rephrase and add information to their responses? Did I repeat the prompt to make sure the children learned from the expansion?

- What types of prompts did I use? How many completion prompts? Recall prompts? Open-ended prompts? Distancing prompts? What, where, when, and how prompts? Count the number of each kind of prompt.

- Which book and print concepts did I teach?
- Which phonological awareness skills did I teach?

Look at your answers to these questions. Set goals for yourself to improve the quality of your storybook reading.

CHAPTER 5

Helping Parents Help Their Children Learn

Although teachers are undeniably influential in promoting young children's literacy growth, parents are essential partners in their children's development of reading, writing, and talking skills. The research on early literacy development suggests not only how teachers can support children's learning in the classroom but also how they can support parents as first teachers at home (Purcell-Gates, 2004; Sulzby & Teale, 1991). Building skilled and confident readers and writers requires collaboration between school and home, teachers, and parents. This chapter discusses a number of ways in which teachers can meet, communicate, and collaborate with parents, including home visits and parent workshops. Next, we present a number of strategies that parents can use to promote their children's literacy learning, including rich talk, language play, interactive storybook reading, and informal instruction about letters and words.

Helping Parents Become "First Teachers"

Parent–teacher interactions provide parents with information on how to support their children's literacy learning and give teachers information on how to extend the children's home-based learning in the classroom. Home visits and parent workshops are two kinds of personal interactions many preschool teachers use.

Home Visits

While some home-visit programs are simply visits to children's homes, others combine home visits with instruction. These programs can have a lasting effect on young children's development. Home-visit programs help parents see themselves as their children's first and most important teachers. Take a look at a typical home visit.

Strategies in Use: Home Visits

Tyrone's teacher visits his home once every other week on Monday. On Tuesday through Thursday, Tyrone plays and learns in a preschool classroom with his teacher and 14 peers. On this Monday, his teacher arrives at his home planning to read *Chicka Chicka Boom Boom* (Martin & Archambault, 1989). She begins by reading the storybook to Tyrone while his grandmother watches. The teacher pauses to focus Tyrone's attention on the pictures, to ask him to predict what might happen next, to invite him to "read" a word with her, and so forth.

Following the reading, she gives Tyrone a sheet of paper, several paper scraps, and some paste to make a collage picture. As Tyrone works at making the collage, the teacher and grandmother talk about his development as a reader and a writer. The teacher asks the grandparent about Tyrone's interest in letters and words. Does he ask her the names of letters and words? Does she help Tyrone notice the letters and words on signs and food packages?

When Tyrone is finished with his collage, the teacher helps him print his name on the paper. Tyrone prints the initial *T* and the teacher writes the rest, announcing the letters as Tyrone watches. She finishes by writing, "Tyrone is a collage artist!" Tyrone displays his artwork on the refrigerator. Finally, the teacher leaves Tyrone and his grandmother with several storybooks and some suggestions for related activities.

For any home-visit program to be successful, the teacher and parents must speak the same language. If the teacher is not conversant in a child's home language, inviting another adult who speaks both the teacher's and the parents' language to assist in the home visit can help to facilitate communication.

Parent Workshops

When teachers teach all day every day, it can be difficult to find time to visit the children's homes. Parent workshops are an efficient way for teachers to meet with families and share suggestions and techniques for supporting children's literacy development at home. During workshops, instead of demonstrating to one parent, the teacher models teaching strategies for everyone in attendance. By providing access to engaging materials and demonstrating how to use them, teachers can help parents become partners in their children's learning.

What topics should workshops address? As we've seen in the previous pages, parents are most effective as first teachers when they concentrate on three goals: talking with children, helping children learn about books and print, and teaching children about letters and words. Effective preschool family workshops should focus on these three goals.

Sponsoring a successful parent workshop requires careful planning. Ask yourself, What activities will work best with these parents? (Remember: Parents are most engaged when they are active participants. Interactive activities are more effective and enjoyable than lectures.) What supplies are needed? How should the meeting room be organized? What time works best for the parents? Are there funds for refreshments? Are name tags needed? Who will provide child care?

Other Ways to Involve Families

No matter how carefully planned the workshop is, not all the children's parents will attend. Therefore, preschool teachers must look for other ways to involve their children's families. Some preschool teachers send letters to their children's homes with specific suggestions for activities parents and children can share (see Figure 7). Some teachers also prepare backpacks with book and learning activities that children can check out for use at home. For example, Cohen (1997) has developed 20 backpacks, each on a different theme, author, or genre (e.g., poetry, nonfiction, memoirs). Topics include folk tales and fairy tales, the post office, birthdays, and more. Each backpack contains books for the children, a book for the parents, and a notebook in which family members can share their thoughts about the book. Parents are encouraged to read the books and talk about them with their children. Carolyn Lingo, another teacher, sends home backpacks that include storybooks with related activities and hands-on materials. For example, one of her backpacks is based on *Mouse Paint* by Ellen Stoll Walsh (1995). It contains small vials of paint and mixing cups, a paintbrush, a smock, and a newspaper to cover the table. A brief note instructs parents to read the book with their child and then to mix the yellow, blue, and red

---

Figure 7
Sample Parent Letter

Dear Merrie,

Have you been wondering why I have been asking the children to bring in an empty cereal box? Well, we are making a classroom display of our favorite cereals. We cut the front from each cereal box and glue it to a piece of posterboard. Every morning we read the names of our favorite cereal. The children are reading environmental print.

What is environmental print? It is the real-life print children see everywhere they look. Environmental print can be found on street signs ("STOP"), store signs ("Pizza Hut"), and food packages ("Cheerios"). Because the location of the print gives clues to its meaning, environmental print is often the first type of print young children can recognize and understand.

Why not take a walk with your child in your neighborhood to look for environmental print? Take along a pad of paper. Sketch the location of the environmental print and write the word just like it appears (e.g., *STOP*). Back home, see how many environmental print words you and your child can read. Staple the pages together and make a cover for your environmental print book. Encourage your child to "read" your special book to you and other family members.

Sincerely,
Carol

---

paints, just like the mice in the book do. Parents and children are encouraged to describe what happened.

Lynn and Carolyn, like many other teachers of young children, clearly know how important families are to their young children's reading, writing, and speaking development. Alone, teachers are challenged to support children's learning. Together, teachers and parents can support each other's efforts to build successful readers.

Strategies for Partnering With Parents

Encourage Parents to Talk With Their Children

Everyday activities offer rich opportunities for vocabulary development when parents take the time to discuss the sights and sounds encountered along the way. For instance, a visit to the produce department of the grocery store can become an impromptu vocabulary lesson when parents explore the sizes, shapes, textures, and names of the various fruits and vegetables. Parents can pose questions such as, What are the differences between Golden Delicious and Macintosh apples? How did the spaghetti squash get its name?

Like a daily vitamin, at least one new vocabulary word a day is a healthy habit. The key is for teachers to help parents understand the importance of talking with their children—to label what they see and discuss how it works. Remember, "Children who do not hear a lot of talk and who are not encouraged to talk themselves often have problems learning to read" (Armbruster, Lehr, & Osborn, 2003).

Encourage Families to Play With Words

When families play word games, they discover that language can be a source of fun. In the beginning, the adult player will need to model the game and provide most of the rhyming words. But over time, as children gain more practice, they will learn to recognize and produce rhymes. Remind families that in rhyming games, sound is more important than meaning. Nonsense words are fine—and children enjoy them most of all. The example that follows illustrates the types of word games parents can play with their children.

• • • • • • • • • • • • • •

Strategies in Use: Encouraging Word Play

A parent and child are riding the bus home. The parent sees a stop sign and points it out to the child.

Parent: What rhymes with *stop*? *Pop, top, mop, bop, hop....* [Before saying each rhyming word, the parent pauses and waits for the child to say the next word. The parent sees a police officer, points, and pauses.]

Child: *Cop!*

Parent: WOW! You made a rhyme! *Cop. Stop.*

Child: *Fop!*

Parent: Wow, are you good at making rhyming words!

• • • • • • • • • • • • • •

Encourage Frequent Storybook Reading

The National Education Goals Panel (1997) stated,

> Early, regular reading to children is one of the most important activities parents can do with their children to improve their readiness for school, serve as their child's first teacher, and instill a love of books and reading. Reading to

children familiarizes them with story components such as characters, plot, action, and sequence ("Once upon at time...," "...and they lived happily ever after"), and helps them associate oral language with printed text. Most important, reading to children builds their vocabularies and background knowledge about the world. (p. 20)

The National Education Goals Panel also reported that only about 56% of 3- to 5-year-olds are read to daily by their parents. To ensure every child's success as a reader, this statistic has to change. Teachers can offer parents many suggestions for activities and reading methods to try during storybook reading. For example, teachers can introduce parents to dialogic reading and the PEER and CROWD procedures described in Chapter 4.

Talk helps young children understand stories and relate them to their own lives. Through discussion, stories become more meaningful.

Encourage Parents to Talk With Their Children While Reading a Story

Talk helps young children understand stories and relate them to their own lives. Through discussion, stories become more meaningful. The following example demonstrates how talk can enrich the read-aloud experience.

• • • • • • • • • • • • • •

Strategies in Use: Parents Talking With Children During Reading

Four-year-old Lauren and her mother are reading *The Biggest, Best Snowman* (Cuyler, 1998). The story begins with Little Nell's family telling her that she can't help because she is too small, so she goes off to play with her friends in the woods. Little Nell's friends ask her to help them build a snowman. Little Nell says that she can't help because she is too small.

Lauren's mother reads the first five pages and stops just after Bear Cub asks Little Nell to show the animals how to make a snowman.

Mother: So, what do you think Little Nell will say?

Lauren: I can't. I'm too little.

Mother: What makes you think Little Nell will say that?

Lauren: Because her name is "Little" Nell.

Mother: But you are little and you can do lots of things, can't you? Could you help the animals make a snowman? Let's see what Little Nell says.

As Mother continues reading, she stops regularly to ask questions and give feedback and to help Lauren connect the story to personal experiences. For example, after the bottom snowball is made, she asks, "What does the snowman need now?" and later, "Do you remember when you and Grandpa made a snowman last winter? Did you make your snowman just like Little Nell and her friends?" But Mother didn't ask all the questions.

Lauren: Why did they make the face using that stuff? What's that [gazed]? What's that [creation]?

And the storybook reading ended with Mother asking the last question:

Mother: So, what do you think BIG Mama, BIG Sarah, and BIG Lizzie learned about Little Nell?

• • • • • • • • • • • • • • •

Through many experiences reading many different kinds of books, Lauren is learning a lot about books and print. She knows how to hold a book. She knows that her mother reads the words in books, not the pictures. She knows that her mother reads the left page before reading the right page. Lauren is developing concepts of print.

Teachers should encourage parents to read to their children the same kinds of books that we recommend for the classroom library corner (see Chapter 4): picture storybooks, predictable books, counting books, and informational books. Parents can begin by taking their children to the local library to take advantage of the many free resources available there.

Encourage Parents to Teach Children About Letters and Words

Children who have had experiences with print understand that the squiggly marks on paper are special; they can be named. Repeated exposure and varied experience are the keys to building alphabet knowledge. Parents can support this learning in many ways. One of the most important ways is by helping children learn the names of the letters of the alphabet, beginning with those letters in the child's name. At the same time, parents should understand that children develop at different rates and that not all children will be able to name the letters of the alphabet by the time they are 5. Adams (1990) suggests beginning with uppercase letters, followed by lowercase letters. Uppercase letters are likely to be more familiar to children because they see more uppercase letters in the world outside the classroom.

Teachers can suggest many simple activities for parents to share with their children, such as singing the alphabet song, looking for letters in street signs and license plates, writing children's names and naming each letter in turn, finding letters in books and newspapers, and reading alphabet books.

Children can begin to recognize words at the same time they are learning about letters; it is not necessary for children to know the names of the letters before they learn to identify highly meaningful words. Teachers might recommend that parents read predictable books with repeated phrases and read these books again and again. While reading, parents should point to the words and encourage their children to chant the repeated phrases with them. In the following scene, Quinn and his father share a bedtime ritual.

• • • • • • • • • • • • • • •

Strategies in Use: Parents Teaching Children About Letters and Words

Quinn's favorite book is *Brown Bear, Brown Bear, What Do You See?* (Martin, 1992). Every night he yells, "Brown Bear, Brown Bear!" to indicate his bedtime reading choice. His father groans; Quinn giggles. His father says, "Okay, but only if you read it with me." Quinn's father reads the "...What do you see?" pages, and Quinn "reads" the "I see a..." pages. His father is often heard to say, "Quinn, you are one heck of a reader!"

• • • • • • • • • • • • • • •

Quinn's enthusiastic reading of *Brown Bear, Brown Bear, What Do You See?* occurred because his father read the book to him many times. The book's repeating pattern supported Quinn's efforts to "read" with and to his father. Such books make it easy for parents to say, "What a good reader you are!"

In Chapter 1, we discussed the importance of children's reading of environmental print (e.g., cereal names, soft drink names, road signs, billboards). Drawing attention to this highly contextualized print is another key way in which parents can support their children's ability to recognize meaningful words. Parents can simply point out salient environmental print during daily activities such as going to the grocery store or going out to eat. Or they can play games with their children, such as "name the traffic sign" or "name the restaurant."

There is one more word of great importance to each preschooler: his or her name. Teachers might encourage parents to print their child's name on a piece of paper and post it above his or her bed, on the refrigerator, and in other visible places in the home. Writing the child's name while he or she watches, saying each letter as it is written, and asking the child to say the letters and read the name will help children begin to recognize this very important word.

Parents play a critical role in nurturing young children's literacy learning. Teachers should reach out to parents to form two-way partnerships aimed at building parents' awareness of the important role they play in their children's literacy learning and providing them with strategies for nurturing their children's early reading, writing, and speaking development.

PROFESSIONAL DEVELOPMENT FOR PRE- AND INSERVICE TEACHERS

This chapter discusses strategies for partnering with parents to enhance children's at-home literacy experiences. Preschool teachers should reach out to parents to form two-way partnerships aimed at building parents' awareness of the important role they play in their children's literacy learning and at providing them with strategies for nurturing their children's early reading, writing, and speaking development.

- Plan a workshop that encourages parents to engage in conversations with their children while reading a story and to teach their children about letters and words. Write a letter to invite parents to the workshop. List the supplies you will need. If you are currently teaching, offer your workshop to a group of parents.

- Write a monthly newsletter that contains specific suggestions for several literacy activities that parents and children can share.

CHAPTER 6

New Challenges, New Opportunities

Today's preschool teachers and preschool children face new challenges and new opportunities. Recall the description of the research that supports developmentally appropriate reading, writing, and talking strategies presented in Chapter 1. The emergent literacy researchers of the 1980s and 1990s revealed how children observe print and its uses in everyday life, test their ideas, and revise them according to the feedback they receive from supportive parents and teachers. These researchers discovered how critical it is for teachers and parents to read frequently to children; to engage them in conversations about text, print, and books; and to provide opportunities for them to observe and interact with adults and other children as they write for real-life purposes. They learned that with repeated opportunities to engage in meaningful literacy activities, a great deal of interaction with adults and peers, and some incidental instruction, many children become conventional readers and writers.

Findings from research on emergent literacy challenged preschool teachers to ask themselves questions such as the following:

- Do I read to my students frequently?
- When I read, do I engage the children in talk about the stories and the print?
- How often do the children see me reading and writing? Am I modeling a variety of forms of literacy for the children?
- Am I providing the children with opportunities to use reading and writing materials in the classroom?
- As the children test their ideas about how print works, do I provide them with supportive feedback that helps them revise their ideas?
- Do I give children the time they need to interact with me, other adults, and one another in meaningful literacy activities?

Teachers who can answer these questions with a yes are providing their young learners with opportunities to engage in meaningful reading and writing activities.

But this is only the beginning. As discussed in Chapter 1, another group of researchers has also been studying young children's literacy skills and the related appropriate classroom instruction practices. Because of the research methods used by this second group, their work has come to be known as scientifically based reading research (SBRR). These SBRR researchers concluded that to become successful readers and writers, children first needed to master the skills necessary for processing print. This research enriched the emergent literacy research findings by identifying the core knowledge and skills that young children must have to become successful readers. The work of Whitehurst (1992) and other researchers revealed that children's oral language skills, phonological awareness, and alphabet knowledge at preschool age are predictive of their reading achievement in the elementary grades. This research suggested that there is a sequence in children's acquisition of phonological awareness and that print knowledge, which includes concepts of print, is positively correlated with children's reading ability in the primary grades.

Findings from SBRR challenged preschool teachers to ask themselves the following questions:

- Am I providing the children with opportunities to learn the names of the letters of the alphabet?
- Do I engage in word play with the children, helping them learn that oral language is composed of words and that words consist of syllables and sounds?
- Do I systematically teach children the meanings of new words?
- Do I help children focus on the sounds of words so that they become familiar with rhyme and alliteration?

If preschool teachers are to provide successful early literacy instruction, they must first understand what skills and experiences young children need to become successful readers and writers.

The SBRR also identified effective strategies for teaching these core literacy skills to young children. One of the most consistent research findings is that young children's phonological awareness and alphabet knowledge can be increased through explicit instruction. In the past, preschool teachers typically have not used explicit instruction with young children. Here, then, is a new challenge. Fortunately, it is possible for this instruction to take the form of games and other developmentally appropriate activities.

(See, for example, the Strategies in Use vignette later in this chapter with the description of Jodie's music activity that teaches letter names.)

It is clear that both the emergent literacy and SBRR perspectives make significant contributions to a well-rounded early literacy program. Children need many meaningful, social engagements with books, various forms of print, and writing. In addition, most children also need some explicit, developmentally appropriate instruction on phonological awareness, letter recognition, and vocabulary. Teachers, therefore, need to know and use instructional strategies from both perspectives.

But doing everything that is proposed in this book is only a beginning. Even teachers who provide all the right elements—literacy-rich classroom environments, play-related literacy activities, interactive storybook reading, appropriate forms of explicit instruction, and family literacy activities—face another challenge. Teachers need to provide their young learners with opportunities to learn the key literacy skills while studying meaningful topics. Children need to learn content—new information about the world—at the same time that they are learning literacy skills.

Selecting Meaningful Topics

Teachers need to carefully select a topic of study and then consider ways to use that topic as a springboard for teaching key literacy concepts. For example, during instruction on a theme such as vehicles, although children think they are simply studying vehicles, teachers know they are also learning about the names of vehicles, how vehicles make our lives better, and the challenges vehicles create. In addition, children are learning that print is read from left to right and from top to bottom, that words are made up of letters, and that some words have rhyming sounds. (Take a moment to re-read Debbie Helman's shared reading of *Tabby Tiger, Taxi Driver* in Chapter 4. Debbie's reading of this Big Book occurred during the classroom's transportation unit. Note how she wove the teaching of literacy into the reading of the Big Book.) The challenge is to select topics that interest young children and to integrate literacy activities into the study of every meaningful topic.

> Teachers need to carefully select a topic of study and then consider ways to use that topic as a springboard for teaching key literacy concepts.

How do preschool teachers make the right decisions about which topics are "meaningful" for young children? Katz and Chard (1989) suggest that teachers use relevance to children's daily lives as the criteria to select topics appropriate for young children's study. Using this advice, Wellhousen (1996) chose to study homes with her young learners: Who lives in them, things to do at home, different kinds of home structures, different types of homes, different locations, and parts of homes. Susan Humphries of the Coombes County Infant School in Arborfield Cross, England, chose to study native plants with her young students. The children actively investigated the life cycle of numerous plants, from the planting to the harvesting and eating. Nancy Edwards of the Preschool Laboratory on the University of Delaware's campus in Newark, Delaware, USA, and her students studied ponds, watching tadpoles turn into frogs and the pond animals and plants awaken after the long winter.

Investigations like these help young children make sense of the world in which they live. Furthermore, they create a powerful context for meaningful reading, writing, and conversation. It is natural for children's vocabulary to grow through such studies. The challenge for the preschool teacher is to weave explicit teaching of key literacy skills into everyday activities.

• • • • • • • • • • • • • •

Strategies in Use: Selecting Meaningful Topics

Mindful teachers ask questions and make decisions such as these:

- While I'm reading to the children today, which print awareness skills will I focus on? Perhaps I'll use a Big Book and focus on print going from left to right across the page.

- As we name the different kinds of transportation we know today, should I focus on the names of the letters in one vehicle? I think I'll focus on the *T* in *Taxi*. We'll find all the uppercase *T*s in the book. I'll make a chart and record the number of *T*s we find on each page. I'll ask the children to read the chart to see which page had the most *T*s on it and the least *T*s on it.

- There are lots of words that begin with the /t/ sound in this book. Today I'll focus on alliteration and ask the children to name all the things they can think of that begin like *Tabby*, *tiger*, and *taxi*. I'll point out that *Tamara* begins just like *Tabby*, *tiger*, and *taxi*.

- While I'm reading today, which words might not have meaning for my children?

- The children ride the bus, but I wonder if they have ever ridden in a taxi. Will they know the difference between a taxi and a "regular" car? I think I'll see if I can get a taxi to come to the center tomorrow. I'll put my car beside the taxi and ask the children to tell me what's different and what's the same. I'll try to focus their attention on the meter and special taxi driver license, which my car doesn't have. Then, to drive the cars in the block corner tomorrow will require a taxi driver license, which they can make in the writing center.

Without such careful planning, integration of literacy skills into the study of meaningful topics might not happen. This is a challenge that every preschool teacher faces.

• • • • • • • • • • • • • • •

Meeting All Children's Needs

Early childhood classrooms today are more diverse than at any time in the past. In addition to children with special needs, early childhood classrooms are increasingly culturally, ethnically, and linguistically diverse. According to the U.S. Census Bureau, by 2030, children of European American families will make up less than 50% of the population under age 5 (see www.census.gov). Early childhood classrooms in some states, like California, already are experiencing this shift toward increased diversity in preschool and nursery programs. In 2006, for example, 56 languages were spoken by children and their families in California (California Department of Education, 2006).

These new demographics challenge preschool teachers to ask themselves questions like the following:

- What am I doing to form meaningful partnerships with my children's families? How do I show that I recognize and respect families' language beliefs and practices? Have I acquired information on how my children's families engage in the use of language and literacy in their homes?

- What do I know about how my children's families use language and how do my teaching practices incorporate the linguistic and cultural resources that children bring with them so that I am promoting my children's learning?

- Can my children relate to the content being presented? How do I support my children's use of their home language while they are acquiring English?

- Do I design and implement activities that promote language use as children engage in individual and group activities?

- Do I encourage my children to experiment with the use, form, purpose, and intent of their home and the English language?

- Do I support my children's continued acquisition of their home language as they acquire English as a second language?

- Do I recognize that code switching is a normal part of language development for many bilingual children?

- Do I offer a variety of opportunities for my children to explore written materials as well as the sounds of the spoken language through rhyme and alliterations?

The California Department of Education (2007) suggests that attention to these kinds of questions is essential for English-language learners' immediate and future learning outcomes. To assist the state's teachers in better serving the needs of preschool English-language learners, the Department of Education prepared a helpful resource guide titled *Preschool English Language Learners: Principles and Practices to Promote Language, Literacy, and Learning*. Readers might wish to write to the California Department of Education in Sacramento, California, USA, for a copy of this guide.

Standards, Instruction, and Assessment

A growing body of research informs early childhood educators about what children need to know before coming to kindergarten if they are to be successful readers and writers. Some of this research is referenced in this book. In 2002, the U.S. federal government launched an early childhood initiative known as Good Start, Grow Smart (see www.whitehouse.gov/infocus/earlychildhood/toc.html). At the heart of Good Start, Grow Smart was the concern that not all young children are receiving quality education and care, not even those young children in federally supported preschool programs. This initiative encourages states to use this body of research to develop voluntary guidelines (or standards) on language and prereading skills for children ages 3 to 5 that align with each state's K–12 standards. States heeded this call and pulled committees of teachers, parents, administrators, and higher education faculty together to establish oral language and early literacy standards. These standards defined what young children should know and be able to do by the time they left preschool for kindergarten.

Teachers, then, used these standards to guide their decisions about what to teach in their classrooms.

• • • • • • • • • • • • • • •

Strategies in Use: Using Standards to Guide Decision Making

It's September, and Jodie, a newly hired Head Start teacher in Virginia, is as excited and nervous as her 4-year-old students. In preparation for her children's arrival, Jodie read everything the center director gave her. One document was *Virginia's Foundation Blocks for Early Learning: Guidelines for Literacy and Mathematics* (Virginia Department of Education, 2003). She read that the purpose of the Virginia standards document was "to provide early childhood educators a set of basic guidelines in literacy and mathematics with indicators of success for entering kindergarteners based on scientifically based research" and that the guidelines had been aligned with the state's kindergarten standards. She carefully studied each of the **specific indicators**—outcomes such as, the child can successfully

- Detect beginning sounds in words
- Listen to 2 one-syllable words and blend them together to form the compound word
- Identify words that rhyme
- Generate simple rhymes

One of the Virginia standards specifies that by the end of preschool children should be able to demonstrate that they can correctly identify 10 to 18 uppercase alphabet letters by name in random order. Jodie knows that she needs to plan activities that provide her young learners with the opportunity to learn the names of the letters of the alphabet. She also knows that she wants the activities she provides to be developmentally appropriate for her young learners. Virginia's Foundation Blocks for Early Learning suggests a music activity that provides Jodie's students with an opportunity to learn the names of the letters of the alphabet.

Jodie begins by making large letter cards on 8 ½ × 11-inch paper. She prints 1 letter (both upper- and lowercase) on each card. Because there are 15 children in her group, she selects 15 of the large letter cards. Because she knows that the letters in their names are the most important letters to young children, the 15 letters include the first letter in each student's name.

Jodie places the letter cards in a circle on the floor. She tells the children that she will be playing music. While the music is playing, they are to march around the letter cards. When the music stops, each child is to stop and pick up a card. Each child will show the card to the group and say the name of the letter. Jodie and her aide do a quick demonstration of how the game is played.

The music begins, the children march, the music stops, and the children stop and pick up the letter in front of them. Each child shows the letter to the group and says or guesses its name. To keep the activity fresh, she reviews only a few letter names in each round. Then, the children put the letter cards back on the floor, and the music begins again.

• • • • • • • • • • • • • • • •

Notice the playfulness of the activity described in the vignette. Early educators have long invited children to march to music. Today, early educators like Jodie are encouraged to embed what their students need to know and be able to do into typical early childhood activities. By infusing old activities with new content, preschool teachers can provide developmentally appropriate opportunities for children to develop the knowledge and skills addressed in performance standards.

Teachers also used the standards to guide their assessment of their children's language and literacy growth. Most of the assessments that early educators use are **informal assessments** rather than **formal assessments**. In fact, the International Reading Association and National Association for the Education of Young Children (1998) position statement on developmentally appropriate practices for young children suggests that

early reading and writing cannot simply be measured as a set of narrowly defined skills on standardized tests. These measures often are not reliable or valid indicators of what children can do in typical practice, nor are they sensitive to language variations, culture, or experiences of young children. Rather, a sound assessment should be anchored in real-life writing and reading tasks and continuously chronicle a wide range of children's literacy activities in different situations. (p. 14)

Assess, Plan, Teach

Early childhood teachers, like their elementary colleagues, have begun to be consumers of data, their children's data. They assess using a variety of ongoing assessment tools. They study their children's performance on these instruments and their observation data to understand what they should teach next. They plan—large group, small group, and center time activities— to meet their children's diverse needs.

Simply gathering information, of course, is not sufficient. Teachers must make sense of the data. Teachers must make professional judgments about the child's learning and development. The key questions are, "Is the child making progress toward meeting the standards?" and "What can the child do today that he or she could not do before?"

Teachers assess children so that they are able to plan instruction that will meet the needs of each child.

> Teachers assess children so that they are able to plan instruction that will meet the needs of each child.

• • • • • • • • • • • • • • •

Strategies in Use: Using Assessment to Plan Instruction

Jodie studied the checklist and made a list of the children who seemed to know the name of the initial letter in their first name. She then made a list of the children who seemed not to know the letter name. She made a special note about José and Martha. During the activity, she recalled that they would look at their card and say, "Boy!" or "Three." Jodie's tentative judgment was that they did not know the names of the letters of the alphabet, nor did they understand the concept of alphabet letters. She then began to plan alphabet activities that would be appropriate for all her young learners. She planned some group activities like the music activity. She planned to put some alphabet games into the manipulative center and to invite small groups of children to play these games with her during activity time.

• • • • • • • • • • • • • • •

Where to Go From Here?

The greatest challenges bring forth the greatest opportunities: to understand and use effective literacy teaching strategies while engaging children in exciting, meaningful investigations; to integrate essential literacy skills into every aspect of the curriculum; and to begin to link standards, content, and assessment in a mindful, developmentally appropriate manner. This book sets forth the foundations. The rest is up to you.

PROFESSIONAL DEVELOPMENT FOR PRE- AND INSERVICE TEACHERS

Throughout this book, we have stressed the importance of explicitly teaching language and literacy skills within the context of topics that are meaningful to the children. If you are currently teaching, what topic are you and your children currently studying? What language and early reading skills are you teaching within the context of this topic? How are you assessing your children's learning of these skills and content? Are you meeting the challenge of incorporating the findings of scientifically based research into their explicit teaching of language and literacy skills? If you are not yet teaching, visit a nearby preschool classroom to ask the teacher these questions. Is the teacher you interviewed meeting this challenge?

Suggested Materials for Thematic Play Settings

Home Center
- Babysitter instruction forms
- Children's books
- Cookbooks, recipe box
- Junk mail
- Magazines, newspapers
- Message board
- Notepads
- Pencils, pens, markers
- Product containers from children's homes
- Sticky notes
- Telephone book
- Telephone message pads

Business Office
- Calendar
- Computer keyboard and monitor
- File folders
- Notepads
- Order forms
- Pencils, pens, markers
- Stationery, envelopes, stamps
- Telephone message pads
- Typewriter
- Wall signs (e.g., "Please Sign In")

Restaurant
- Cookbooks
- Menus
- Notepads/order pads
- Pencils, pens, markers
- Price chart
- Product containers
- Receipts
- Telephone book
- Wall signs (e.g., "Pay Here")

Post Office
- Address labels
- Baskets labeled "First Class," "Third Class," and "Air Mail"
- Junk mail
- Pencils, pens, markers
- Stamps
- Stationery and envelopes
- Wall signs (e.g., "Line Starts Here")

Grocery Store

- Checkbooks
- Notepads
- Pencils, pens, markers
- Product containers
- Shelf labels for store areas (e.g., "Meat")
- Wall signs (e.g., "Supermarket")

Veterinarian's Office

- Appointment book
- Labels with pets' names
- Magazines
- Pamphlets
- Pencils, pens, markers
- Pet care chart
- Prescription forms
- Telephone book
- Wall signs (e.g., "Receptionist," "Waiting Room," "The Doctor Is In")

Airport/Airplane

- Air sickness bags with printed instructions
- Books, magazines
- Calendar
- Luggage tags
- Maps
- Pencils, pens, markers
- Tickets
- Travel poster
- Wall signs (e.g., "Baggage Claim Area")

Library

- Books
- Library cards
- Pencils, pens, markers
- Shelf labels for books (e.g., "ABCs," "Animals")
- Wall signs (e.g., "Quiet!")

Preschool Standards

Oral Language (Standard)
Areas and Indicators

Gestural Expression

- Uses gestures alone to communicate
- Uses gestures in combination with speech to communicate

Verbal Expression

- Expresses feelings, needs, and ideas
- Uses language to maintain relationships with others
- Participates in conversation
- Asks questions, explains, and gives directions
- Helps generate and maintain scripts in sociodramatic play

Vocabulary and Background Knowledge

- Uses new words encountered in stories in retellings
- Uses new words from book or other contexts in conversations
- Asks for names of unfamiliar objects and their parts
- Asks, "What does that mean?" when hears unfamiliar word
- Understands relationships among objects (e.g., apples and oranges are fruits; socks and dresses are items of clothing)
- Understands processes and properties associated with objects, animals, and plants (e.g., plants and animals grow; rocks do not grow)

Adapted from Schickedanz, J. (2004). Distinguished educator: The role of literacy in early childhood education. ("A framework and suggested guidelines for prekindergarten content standards"), *The Reading Teacher*, 58(1), 86–100.
State Standards Reviewed: Alabama, Arkansas, Colorado, Connecticut, Georgia, Illinois, Louisiana, Massachusetts, Missouri, New Jersey, Ohio, Pennsylvania, Texas
Standards listed represent accomplishments (i.e., what children should know and be able to do) by the end of the preschool period (i.e., at age 5 to 5½).

Listening (Attention to and Comprehension of Talk)

• Responds to name when called

• Attends to stories read aloud

• Follows directions

• Responds to verbal cues from partner in sociodramatic play

• Takes turns in conversation and relates own comments to topic

Phonological Awareness

• Learns quickly to recite interesting-sounding words from texts (e.g., "oonga boonga" and "bunka wunka") and expresses delight in playing with such words

• Thinks of a word that rhymes with a word the adult provides

• Thinks of a word that starts with the same sound as a word the adult provides

• Segments first sound in a word when teacher asks, "What's the first sound we hear in bird?" (Child: "/b/."), or when the child is writing words (e.g., Child: *Birthday. /b/.*)

Literacy (Standard)

Areas and Indicators

Print Awareness

• Asks what words in books and in the environment say

• Indicates meaning for marks created when writing

Print Conventions and Book Handling Knowledge

• Holds books right side up and proceeds from front to back

• Looks at left page before right page when going through a book

• Knows cover of book and that title of book is found there

• Runs finger left to right and top to bottom when "reading" print

Letter-Name Knowledge

• Names many uppercase letters

• Knows the lowercase form of all letters in own name

• Finds specific letters in words in the environment (signs, book titles, and so on)

Alphabetic Principle

- Attempts to sound out print in the environment
- Attempts to sound out words and to spell them (can isolate first letter)
- Tells adults, "*A* is for *acorn*" or "*B* is for *banana*"

Knowledge of Text Structures

- Names different kinds of texts (recipes, menus, signs, newspapers, greeting cards, letters, storybooks)
- Relates events from familiar narrative texts, in sequence
- Seeks information from nonfiction texts
- Generates stories with basic story structure in dramatic play and when dictating stories at writing center

Comprehension of Stories

- Names main characters when asked, "Who is in this story?"
- Retells a story by enacting roles in play or with puppets
- Retells stories using book as prompt
- Relates some main events when asked, "What happens in this story?"
- Relates book experiences to own life (e.g., "I am going to make angels in the snow, just like Peter.")
- Uses own experiences to understand characters' feelings and motivations
- Uses background knowledge to interpret story events
- Links basic emotions of characters to their actions in story events

Interest in Books

- Chooses often to look at books in book area
- Checks out books from classroom lending library
- Requests that favorite stories be read
- Looks at information books provided in the science or the block area
- Demonstrates sustained and focused engagement during story time

Beginning Writing

- Writes for many purposes (signs, labels, stories, messages)
- Frequently chooses writing area
- Uses writing in blocks and dramatic play contexts

- Writes own name, using good approximations to letters needed
- Makes mock and actual letters and experiments with letter forms
- Organizes writing linearly on a writing surface and goes from left to right and from top to bottom
- Uses two kinds of letters when writing: "big" ones and "little" ones
- Composes messages and dictates or writes these
- Contributes to class writing projects
- Experiments with making words by stringing letters together to look like words or by attempting to link sounds in words to specific letter names

REFERENCES

Adams, M.J. (1990). *Beginning to read: Thinking and learning about print*. Cambridge, MA: MIT Press.

Adams, M.J., Foorman, B.R., Lundberg, I., & Beeler, T. (1998). The elusive phoneme: Why phonemic awareness is so important and how to help children develop it. *American Educator, 22*(1–2), 18–29.

Aram, D. (2006). Early literacy interventions: The relative roles of storybook reading, alphabetic activities, and their combination. *Reading and Writing, 19*(5), 489–515. doi:10.1007/s11145-006-9005-2

Armbruster, B.B., Lehr, F., & Osborn, J. (2003). *A child becomes a reader: Birth through preschool: Proven ideas from research for parents* (2nd ed.). Portsmouth, NH: RMC Research Corporation.

Arnold, D.H., Lonigan, C.J., Whitehurst, G.J., & Epstein, J.N. (1994). Accelerating language development through picture book reading: Replication and extension to a videotape training format. *Journal of Educational Psychology, 86*(2), 235–243. doi:10.1037/0022-0663.86.2.235

Baghban, M. (1984). *Our daughter learns to read and write: A case study from birth to three*. Newark, DE: International Reading Association.

Barker, R. (1978). *Habitats, environments, and human behavior*. San Francisco: Jossey-Bass.

Barrentine, S.J. (1996). Engaging in reading through interactive read-alouds. *The Reading Teacher, 50*(1), 36–43.

Beauchat, K. (2008). *Making the most of shared reading in preschool*. Unpublished executive position paper, University of Delaware, Newark.

Beck, I.J., & McKeown, M.G. (2007). Increasing young low-income children's oral vocabulary repertoires through rich and focused instruction. *The Elementary School Journal, 107*(3), 251–271. doi:10.1086/511706

Beck, I.J., McKeown, M.G., & Kucan, L. (2002). *Bringing words to life: Robust vocabulary instruction*. New York: Guilford.

Biemiller, A. (2005). Size and sequence in vocabulary development: Implications for choosing words for primary grade vocabulary instruction. In E.H. Hiebert & M.L. Kamil (Eds.), *Teaching and learning vocabulary* (pp. 223–242). Mahwah, NJ: Erlbaum.

Biemiller, A., & Slonim, N. (2001). Estimating root word vocabulary growth in normative and advantaged populations: Evidence for a common sequence of vocabulary acquisition. *Journal of Educational Psychology, 93*(3), 498–520. doi:10.1037/0022-0663.93.3.498

Bruner, J. (1983). Play, thought, and language. *Peabody Journal of Education, 60*(3), 60–69.

Bruner, J. (1984). Language, mind, and reading. In H. Goelman, A. Oberg, & F. Smith (Eds.), *Awakening to literacy* (pp. 193–200). Portsmouth, NH: Heinemann.

Bus, A.G., van IJzendoorn, M.H., & Pellegrini, A.D. (1995). Joint book reading makes for success in learning to read: A meta-analysis on intergenerational transmission of literacy. *Review of Educational Research, 65*(1), 1–21.

California Department of Education. (2006). *Fact book 2006: Handbook of education information*. Sacramento: Author.

California Department of Education. (2007). *Preschool English learners: Principles and practices to promote language, literacy, and learning*. Sacramento: Author.

Calkins, L.M. (1994). *The art of teaching writing*. Portsmouth, NH: Heinemann.

Christie, J.F. (2008). The scientifically based reading research approach to early literacy instruction. In L.M. Justice & C. Vukelich (Eds.), *Achieving excellence in preschool literacy instruction* (pp. 25–40). New York: Guilford.

Christie, J.F., & Wardle, F. (1992). How much time is needed for play? *Young Children, 47*(3), 28–33.

Clark, M.M. (1976). *Young fluent readers: What can they teach us?* London: Heinemann.

Clay, M. (1966). *Emergent reading behavior*. Unpublished doctoral dissertation, University of Auckland, New Zealand.

Cohen, L.E. (1997). How I developed my kindergarten book backpack program. *Young Children, 52*(2), 69–71.

Dale, E., & Chall, J.S. (1948). A formula for predicting readability and instructions. *Educational Research Bulletin, 27*, 11–20, 28.

Dale, E., & O'Rourke, J. (1981). The living word vocabulary: A national vocabulary inventory. Chicago: World Book/Childcraft International.

DeLong, A.J., Tegano, D.W., Moran, J.D., Brickey, J., Morrow, D., & Houser, T.L. (1994). Effects of spatial scale on cognitive play in preschool children. *Early Education and Development, 5*(3), 237–246. doi:10.1207/s15566935eed0503_5

Dickinson, D.K., McCabe, A., Anastasopoulos, L., Peisner-Feinberg, E.S., & Poe, M.D. (2003). The comprehensive language approach to early literacy: The interrelationships among vocabulary, phonological sensitivity, and print knowledge among preschool-aged children. *Journal of Educational Psychology, 95*(3), 465–481. doi:10.1037/0022-0663.95.3.465

Dickinson, D.K., & Snow, C.E. (1987). Interrelationships among prereading and oral language skills in kindergartners from two social classes. *Early Childhood Research Quarterly, 2*(1), 1–25. doi:10.1016/0885-2006(87)90010-X

Dolch, E.W. (1948). *Problems in reading*. Champaign, IL: Garrard Press.

Duke, N.K. (2000). 3.6 minutes per day: The scarcity of informational texts in first grade. *Reading Research Quarterly, 35*(2), 202–224. doi:10.1598/RRQ.35.2.1

Duke, N.K., & Kays, J. (1998). "Can I say 'Once upon a time'?": Kindergarten children developing knowledge of information book language. *Early Childhood Research Quarterly, 13*(2), 295–318. doi:10.1016/S0885-2006(99)80041-6

Durkin, D. (1966). *Children who read early: Two longitudinal studies*. New York: Teachers College Press.

Ehri, L.C., & Roberts, T. (2006). The roots of learning to read and write: Acquisition of letters and phonemic awareness. In D.K. Dickinson & S.B. Neuman (Eds.), *Handbook of early literacy research* (Vol. 2, pp. 113–131). New York: Guildford.

Enz, B., & Christie, J.F. (1997). Teacher play interaction styles: Effects on play behavior and relationships with teacher training and experience. *International Journal of Early Childhood Education, 2,* 55–69.

Ericson, L., & Juliebö, M.F. (1998). *The phonological awareness handbook for kindergarten and primary teachers.* Newark, DE: International Reading Association.

Ezell, H.K., & Justice, L.M. (2005). *Shared storybook reading: Building young children's language and emergent literacy skills.* Baltimore: Paul H. Brookes.

Fractor, J.S., Woodruff, M.C., Martinez, M.G., & Teale, W.H. (1993). Let's not miss opportunities to promote voluntary reading: Classroom libraries in the elementary school. *The Reading Teacher, 46*(6), 476–484.

Fuchs, D., & Fuchs, L.S. (2006). Introduction to Response to Intervention: What, why, and how valid is it? *Reading Research Quarterly, 41*(1), 93–99. doi:10.1598/RRQ.41.1.4

Gambrell, L.B. (2000, April). *Fostering comprehension.* Paper presented at the 45th annual convention of the International Reading Association, Indianapolis, IN.

Han, M., & Christie, J. (2001). Environmental factors in play: Space, materials, and time. *International Journal of Early Childhood Education, 7,* 149–162.

Hemmeter, M.L., Ostrosky, M.M., Artman, K., & Kinder, K. (2008). Moving right along: Planning transitions to prevent challenging behaviors. *Young Children, 63*(3), 18–25.

Holdaway, D. (1979). *The foundations of literacy.* Sydney; New York: Ashton Scholastic.

International Reading Association & National Association for the Education of Young Children. (1998). *Learning to read and write: Developmentally appropriate practices for young children.* Newark, DE; Washington, DC: Author.

Johnson, J.E., Christie, J.F., & Wardle, F. (2005). *Play, development, and early education.* New York: Allyn & Bacon.

Justice, L.M., Bowles, R.P., & Skibbe, L.E. (2006). When are print concepts learned? A study of typical and at-risk 3- to 5-year-old children. *Language, Speech, and Hearing Services in Schools, 37*(3), 224–235. doi:10.1044/0161-1461(2006/024)

Justice, L.M., & Ezell, H.K. (2000). Enhancing children's print and word awareness through home-based parent intervention. *American Journal of Speech-Language Pathology, 9*(3), 257–269.

Justice, L.M., Meier, J., & Walpole, S. (2005). Learning new words from storybooks: An efficacy study with at-risk kindergarteners. *Language, Speech, and Hearing Services in Schools, 36*(1), 17–32. doi:10.1044/0161-1461(2005/003)

Katz, L.G., & Chard, S.C. (1989). *Engaging children's minds: The project approach.* Norwood, NJ: Ablex.

Lonigan, C. (2008, April). *(Almost) everything you wanted to know about phonological awareness and were afraid to ask.* Paper presented at Early Reading First Conference, New Orleans, LA.

McGee, L.M. (2007). *Transforming literacy practices in preschool: Research-based practices that give all children the opportunity to reach their potential as learners*. New York: Scholastic.

McGee, L.M., Lomax, R., & Head, M. (1988). Young children's written language knowledge: What environmental and functional print reading reveals. *Journal of Reading Behavior, 20*(2), 99–118.

Morrow, L.M. (2009). *Literacy development in the early years: Helping children read and write* (6th ed.). Boston: Allyn & Bacon.

National Education Goals Panel. (1997). *Special early childhood report*. Washington, DC: Author.

National Institute of Child Health and Human Development. (2000). *Report of the National Reading Panel. Teaching children to read: An evidence-based assessment of the scientific research literature on reading and its implications for reading instruction* (NIH Publication No. 00-4769). Washington, DC: U.S. Government Printing Office.

Neuman, S.B. (2002). What research reveals: Foundations for reading instruction in preschool and primary education. Washington, DC: U.S. Department of Education.

Neuman, S.B., & Roskos, K.A. (1992). Literacy objects as cultural tools: Effects on children's literacy behaviors in play. *Reading Research Quarterly, 27*(3), 202–225.

Neuman, S.B., & Roskos, K.A. (2005). Viewpoint: Whatever happened to developmentally appropriate practice in early literacy? *Young Children, 60*(4), 22–26.

Neuman, S.B., & Roskos, K.A. (2007). *Nurturing knowledge: Building a foundation for school success by linking early literacy to math, science, art, and social studies*. New York: Scholastic.

Ostrosky, M.M., Jung, E.Y., & Hemmeter, M.L. (2008). *Helping children make transitions between activities* (What Works Briefs #4). Retrieved June 4, 2008, from www.vanderbilt.edu/csefel/briefs/wwb4.html

Pearson, P.D., & Gallagher, M.C. (1983). The instruction of reading comprehension. *Contemporary Educational Psychology, 8*(3), 317–344. doi:10.1016/0361-476X(83)90019-X

Pianta, R.C., La Paro, K.M., & Hamre, B.K. (2008). *Classroom Assessment Scoring System: Manual K–3*. Baltimore: Paul H. Brookes.

Purcell-Gates, V. (2004). Family literacy as the site for emerging knowledge of written language. In B. Wasik (Ed.), *Family literacy handbook* (pp. 101–116). Mahwah, NJ: Erlbaum.

Rayner, K., Foorman, B.R., Perfetti, C.A., Pesetsky, D., & Seidenberg, M.S. (2002, March). How should reading be taught? *Scientific American, 286*, 84–91.

Roskos, K.A. (2008, May). *Efficacy of a vocabulary instruction protocol in preschool programs*. PowerPoint presented at the annual convention of the International Reading Association, Atlanta, GA.

Roskos, K.A., & Christie, J.F. (2004). Examining the play–literacy interface: A critical review and future directions. In E. Zigler, D. Singer, & S. Bishop-Josef (Eds.),

Children's play: The roots of reading (pp. 95–123). Washington, DC: Zero to Three Press.

Roskos, K.A., Ergul, C., Bryan, T., Burstein, K., Christie, J.F., & Han, M. (2008). Who's learning what words and how fast?: Preschoolers' vocabulary growth in an early literacy program. *Journal of Research in Childhood Education, 22,* 275–290.

Roskos, K.A., Tabors, P.O., & Lenhart, L.A. (2009). *Oral language and early literacy in preschool: Talking, reading, and writing* (2nd ed.). Newark, DE: International Reading Association.

Scarborough, H.S., & Dobrich, W. (1994). On the efficacy of reading to preschoolers. *Developmental Review, 14*(3), 245–302. doi:10.1006/drev.1994.1010

Sénéchal, M. (1997). The differential effect of storybook reading on preschoolers' acquisition of expressive and receptive vocabulary. *Journal of Child Language, 24*(1), 123–138. doi:10.1017/S0305000996003005

Sénéchal, M., Thomas, E., & Monker, J.-A. (1995). Individual differences in four-year-olds' ability to learn new vocabulary. *Journal of Educational Psychology, 87*(2), 218–229. doi:10.1037/0022-0663.87.2.218

Smith, P.K., & Connolly, K.J. (1980). *The ecology of preschool behaviour.* Cambridge, England: Cambridge University Press.

Snow, C.E., Burns, M.S., & Griffin P. (Eds.). (1998). *Preventing reading difficulties in young children.* Washington, DC: National Academy Press.

Snow, C.E., & Ninio, A. (1986). The contracts of literacy: What children learn from learning to read books. In W. Teale & E. Sulzby (Eds.), *Emergent literacy: Writing and reading* (pp. 116–138). Norwood, NJ: Ablex.

Sulzby, E. (1985). Children's emergent reading of favorite storybooks: A developmental study. *Reading Research Quarterly, 20*(4), 458–481. doi:10.1598/RRQ.20.4.4

Sulzby, E. (1990). Assessment of emergent writing and children's language while writing. In L.M. Morrow & J.K. Smith (Eds.), *Assessment for instruction in early literacy* (pp. 83–108). Englewood, NJ: Prentice Hall.

Sulzby, E., & Teale, W. (1991). Emergent literacy. In R. Barr, M.L. Kamil, P. Mosenthal, & P.D. Pearson (Eds.), *Handbook of reading research* (Vol. 2, pp. 727–757). White Plains, NY: Longman.

Virginia Department of Education. (2003). *Virginia's foundation blocks for early learning: Comprehensive standards for four-year-olds.* Retrieved February 9, 2004, from www.pen.k12.va.us/VDOE/Instruction/Elem_M/FoundationBlocks.pdf

Vukelich, C., Christie, J.F., & Enz, B. (2007). *Helping young children learn language and literacy: Birth through kindergarten* (2nd ed.). Boston: Pearson/Allyn & Bacon.

Wasik, B.A., & Bond, M.A. (2001). Beyond the pages of a book: Interactive book reading and language development in preschool classrooms. *Journal of Educational Psychology, 93*(2), 243–250. doi:10.1037/0022-0663.93.2.243

Wellhousen, K. (1996). Be it ever so humble: Developing a study of homes for today's diverse society. *Young Children, 52*(1), 72–76.

Wells, G. (1985). *Language development in the preschool years.* New York: Cambridge University Press.

What Works Clearinghouse. (2007). *Dialogic reading* (WWC Intervention Report). Princeton, NJ: Author. Retrieved October 7, 2008, from ies.ed.gov/ncee/wwc/pdf/WWC_Dialogic_Reading_020807.pdf

Whitehurst, G.J. (1992). *How to read to your preschooler*. Paper prepared for the State of Connecticut Commission on Children.

Wien, C.A., & Kirby-Smith, S. (1998). Untiming the curriculum: A case study of removing clocks from the program. *Young Children, 53*(5), 8–13.

Wilder, D.A., Chen, L., Atwell, J., Pritchard, J., & Weinstein, P. (2006). Brief functional analysis and treatment of tantrums associated with transitions in preschool children. *Journal of Applied Behavior Analysis, 39*(1), 103–107. Retrieved June 27, 2008, from www.pubmedcentral.nih.gov /picrender.fcgi?tool=pmcentrez&artid=1389600&blobtype=pdf

Yaden, D.B., Rowe, D.W., & MacGillivray, L. (2000). Emergent literacy: A matter (polyphony) of perspectives. In M.L. Kamil, P.B. Mosenthal, P.D. Pearson, & R. Barr (Eds.), *Handbook of reading research* (Vol. 3, pp. 425–454). Mahwah, NJ: Erlbaum.

Yopp, H.K. (1992). Developing phonemic awareness in young children. *The Reading Teacher, 45*(8), 696–703.

LITERATURE CITED

Ada, A.F., & Campoy, F.I. (2003). *Pío peep! Traditional Spanish nursery rhymes*. New York: HarperCollins.

Aylesworth, J. (2003). *Goldilocks and the three bears*. New York: Scholastic.

Baker, L.A. (2003). *The animal ABC*. New York: Henry Holt.

Child, L. (2000). *I will never NOT ever eat a tomato*. Cambridge, MA: Candlewick.

Chodos-Irvine, M. (2003). *Ella Sarah gets dressed*. San Diego, CA: Harcourt.

Cobb, V. (2003). *I face the wind*. New York: HarperCollins.

Cowley, J. (2001). *Tabby Tiger, taxi driver*. Bothell, WA: Wright Group.

Cox, J. (2003). *My family plays music*. New York: Holiday House.

Crews, D. (1997). *Truck*. New York: Tupelo.

Cuyler, M. (1998). *The biggest, best snowman*. New York: Scholastic.

dePaola, T. (1977). *The quicksand book*. New York: Holiday House.

Edwards, P.D. (1998). *Warthogs in the kitchen: A sloppy counting book*. New York: Hyperion.

Gibbons, G. (1988). *Tool book*. New York: Holiday House.

Greenfield, E. (1978). *Honey, I love*. New York: HarperCollins.

Jay, A. (2003). *ABC: A child's first alphabet book*. New York: Dutton.

Jenkins, S., & Page, R. (2003). *What do you do with a tail like this?* Boston: Houghton Mifflin.

Lehn, B. (2002). *What is an artist?* Brookfield, CT: Millbrook.

Martin, B., Jr. (1992). *Brown bear, brown bear, what do you see?* New York: Henry Holt.

Martin, B., Jr, & Archambault, J. (1989). *Chicka chicka boom boom*. New York: Simon & Schuster.

Morales, Y. (2003). *Just a minute: A trickster tale and counting book*. San Francisco: Chronicle.

Moses, W. (2003). *Will Moses' Mother Goose*. New York: Philomel.

Murphy, M. (2003). *I kissed the baby*. Cambridge, MA: Candlewick.

Pearson, D. (2003). *Alphabeep: A zipping, zooming ABC*. New York: Holiday House.

Recorvits, H. (2003). *My name is Yoon*. New York: Farrar, Straus & Giroux.

Rohmann, E. (2002). *My friend rabbit*. Brookfield, CT: Roaring Brook.

Scarry, R. (1999). *Best Mother Goose ever!* New York: Golden.

Sendak, M. (1962). *Chicken soup with rice: A book of months*. New York: HarperCollins.

Smith, W.J. (2003). *Up the hill and down: Poems for the very young*. Honesdale, PA: Boyds Mills.

Waddell, M. (2003). *Hi, Harry! The moving story of how one slow tortoise slowly made a friend*. Cambridge, MA: Candlewick.

Walsh, E.S. (1995). *Mouse paint*. San Diego, CA: Harcourt.

INDEX

Note: Page numbers followed by *f* and *t* indicate figures and tables, respectively.

P

Q

R